THE
GOD
WHO
CHANGES
LIVES

THE GOD WHO CHANGES LIVES

STORIES FROM ALPHA
THE AMERICAN COLLECTION

Edited by Mark Elsdon-Dew

Alpha

Alpha Resources
Alpha North America

Copyright © 2002, Alpha International, Holy Trinity Brompton, Brompton Road, London SW7 1JA, UK

Published in North America by Alpha North America, 74 Trinity Place, New York, NY 10006.

Cover design by Jeffrey P. Barnes
Cover photo: flag; © 2003 Getty Images; Rubberball
    Productions
Additional cover photos by Amy Hoe

Scripture in this publication is from either the Good News Version © 1976, Second Edition © 1994 by the American Bible Society; or the New International Version, © 1973, 1978, 1984 by the International Bible Society.

ISBN: 1-931808-791

2 3 4 5 6 7 8 9 10 Printing/Year 10 09 08 07 06

EDITOR'S ACKNOWLEDGEMENTS

This book could never have been published without the support and kindness of all the contributors, who not only allowed me to interview them at length about their personal lives, but have checked and re-checked the text. I am enormously grateful to each of them.

I would like to thank Ana Lehmann for all the very hard work she has put into the publication of this book. I would also like to thank Sharon Hayles for her continued help in all matters, and also Jenny Budd and the team in Alpha USA.

"Write down for the coming generation what the Lord has done, so that people not yet born will praise him."

Psalm 102:18

CONTENTS

ALPHA

Many of the contributors to this book make particular reference to the Alpha course, a practical introduction to the Christian faith which has had a remarkable impact on many people's lives. The course has proved so popular that there are now over 23,000 courses running around the world.

INTRODUCTION
BY MARK ELSDON-DEW

The Alpha course—an introduction to Christianity for non-churchgoers—is proving little short of a phenomenon in the church today.

Since the mid-1990s, tens of thousands of churches around the world have made the course a central part of their program in making Christianity accessible to their local communities.

More than four million people have completed the course in that time and hundreds of thousands have come to faith in Jesus Christ or had their faith renewed.

Nowhere is the Alpha course spreading faster than in the United States. Almost every week of every year, an Alpha conference is taking place somewhere in America to train local church leaders to run the course in their environment.

At each of these conferences, a short meeting is held for those delegates who have come to faith on the Alpha course themselves—and that is where almost all the stories in this book have originated.

I have attended scores of these meetings now, and time and again I have listened with interest as people have described what God has done in their lives.

The first three volumes of this series have been stories based in the United Kingdom. This one contains stories from the United States—and shows that God reveals

Himself to people in similar ways all over the world.

My criteria for including a story have remained the same:

1. Is the person telling the story someone whose current lifestyle is such that I can trust their account—and stable enough not to be rocked by the very act of telling their story publicly?
2. Is the story unusual enough, yet real enough, to prompt the reader to accept that something unusual took place which can be attributed to the power and presence of the living God?

There is an account in the Old Testament of four starving men who unwittingly fall upon the abandoned camp of the besieging Syrian army with all its treasures and food there for the taking.

They look around and say to each other, "We have good news and we shouldn't keep it to ourselves," (2 Kings 7:9).

The people who tell their stories in these pages have been courageous enough to re-live difficult times because they share those same instincts. They too have good news and say, "We shouldn't keep it to ourselves."

"It was like living in a dark tunnel that had no light. I felt that God had let me down and betrayed me."

1

THE STORY OF MARJORIE FOOR

One terrible night in 1983, Marjorie Foor held her 15-year-old son, Anthony, in her arms as he died—the victim of a knife attack in the family home. Tragically, his killer was Marjorie's 16-year-old foster son, Gregory. The events of that night were to have a grave impact upon all the family. But God was to intervene many years later.

Our mother made us go to church as children. We were taught that it was our duty to go and that we had to do what God wanted in order to gain God's love. Dad never came. He was a police officer and always seemed to be out taking care of other people instead of being home.

When he was at home, he was very abusive and ordered us around a lot. Mother was the nucleus of our family and kept us together. She used to say, "We all have crosses to bear and he's our cross."

I was one of four sisters, and we have always been close. We took refuge in each other's rooms when we were hurting. Jean was the first to marry, then Elaine, then Anne, and finally me. We all continued to go to church after we married. I married Jim who was from Pennsylvania. He was in the Navy, and we met at the local bowling alley when I accidentally threw the ball at his lane.

We were married in 1962 and had four children—three boys and a girl: Timothy, Thomas, Anthony, and Tina. I stayed at home to look after the children and, around 1981, when they were all teenagers, I decided to go into foster care. I went through a vigorous investigation from the police department, the fire department, and the health department. The only condition I gave them at the time was that I didn't want any children who had experienced drug problems because I was afraid that they might hurt my family.

In the following few years, I took about ten children in—some for only a month or two and others for a year or more. One girl stayed with me for two years. By 1983, I had just one boy, Gregory, living with us. He was 16 and had been living with us for seven months. At that time, our other children were ages 18, 17, 15, and 10.

One weekend during that year, we went to Pennsylvania to see our relatives. When we got home, Anthony and

Gregory wanted to go out to a party at a house nearby, while Thomas was going bowling with a friend. By that time, Timmy had left home to join the Navy. Anthony and Gregory walked to their party, which was about a mile away I guess. They got home a few hours later and that was when I noticed that Anthony seemed a little unsteady on his feet. I said, "Have you been drinking?"

And he said, "Yes."

I followed him upstairs and said to the two of them, "You guys have been drinking. We will not deal with that tonight. We'll talk about it in the morning, when I've had more time to think this through." So I went downstairs and sat down on the couch. I must have dozed off for about 15 minutes when I heard the sound of running upstairs and then the noise of what sounded like fighting. So I ran upstairs, and, all of a sudden, I saw my son lying on the floor at the top. Gregory was standing over him and said, "Tony has cut his own throat." I knew at once he was lying. I looked down and saw Anthony lying there with his throat wide open. So I started screaming and screaming and screaming for my husband to wake up. Then I ran downstairs and grabbed a cloth and put it to my son's throat. I kept on screaming and finally my husband appeared and said, "What the hell is going on?"

I said, "Tony's injured. His throat is cut."

He said, "My God, what has happened?" He ran upstairs and I went to the phone to call for an ambulance. I dialed 911 and was screaming into the phone telling them to hurry up. As I dialed, Greg ran down the stairs and into my bedroom, which was on the lower floor. Minutes later, I heard this, "Kapow!" Greg had found the key of our gun cabinet, got the shells out of a drawer, put them in a double-barrelled shotgun, and shot off half of his face. I dropped the phone, ran into the bedroom, and saw Greg lying on the floor, crawling to my bed, with blood everywhere. He grabbed my pillow and covered his shattered face with it. I immediately ran back to the phone and said, "Send two ambulances."

When the police arrived, I was in the bedroom with Greg telling him, "Greg, hold on, hold on. They are coming to help you." Then I ran back upstairs and took Tony in my arms. I rubbed his back and said, "It's all right, darling. Mother's here. Don't worry. Nothing is going to happen to you." I knew he was dying. When the ambulance people arrived, I went down to meet them. They were shouting, "Who's hurt? Who's hurt?"

I said, "Upstairs," to one and "In the back room" to another.

So one ran upstairs and one went through the back to my bedroom. Within minutes, the one in the bedroom ran out to get some equipment sent in to him. At the same time, the ambulance man upstairs said, "There is nothing I can do about this one up here." Tony was dead. They put Greg on a stretcher and took him away in an ambulance, but they left Tony lying upstairs.

Then the police detectives separated our family. My husband was put in the kitchen, my daughter was in her bedroom downstairs, and I stayed with her. As they started questioning us, our son, Tommy, arrived home from the bowling alley and tried to get into the house. He saw all the policemen and fire engines and ambulances, with neighbors standing around, but the police would not let him come into the house because they said it was the scene of a crime.

I said, "He's my son,"

The police detective said, "I don't care who he is; he's got to stay out of here. If he comes in, I will arrest him."

I said, "How can you do that? He's my son. It's his brother that was killed."

Tommy said, "Who is it?"

I said, "It's Tony. He's dead."

At that Tommy backed off and I said, "Tommy back off. I'll be with you in a little bit."

After that, he ran around the house and snuck in through the back way to the kitchen where my husband was sitting in the kitchen. He sat down with his dad, who explained everything to him. But they wouldn't allow us all to be together until after they had questioned us. We were treated as if we had done it because that was the first thing they thought of. They just didn't know what had happened.

I was with my daughter, but I kept having to go to the bathroom because I was so sick. I was vomiting and had diarrhea because of the shock. They asked us questions, and afterward I said, "I want a priest, I want a priest. Bring a priest." They called information and got a priest from Our Lady of Hope, a Catholic church nearby (not the one we attended), and he came and stayed with us while the men were preparing to take Tony's body out. I heard the body bag being brought down and saw them taking Tony out. I was in a terrible state of shock at that point. The priest started praying, and I thought that I was going to lose it mentally. All I could do was pray the "Our Father," the "Hail Mary" and the "Glory be to the Father." I kept praying them over and over and over, terribly fast, with the priest trying to keep up with me.

After a while I suddenly stopped and felt I was coming back to reality. It was now the early hours of the morning, but I called my sister, Anne, on the phone, and the police interrupted our conversation because they were monitoring all our calls. They wouldn't let me tell her what was wrong, but I said, "I've got to talk to you." She knew something horrible had happened. I said, "I can't explain to you. I just need a place to stay."

My husband and the two children packed a few things and we went to Anne's house. She opened the front door and was counting everybody's heads and said, "Where's Tony? Where's Greg?" That was when I told her what had happened. Apparently, I kept looking at my hands, saying, "I need a shower. There's blood on my hands." But there wasn't any blood at that stage because I had washed myself before leaving the house. I was just so distraught that I went into shutdown.

The hardest thing was telling the various members of my family what had happened. I had to tell my mother, who lived alone, and that was hard. Then we had real trouble getting in touch with Timmy, who was on furlough at the time. Eventually the Red Cross tracked him down a day and a half later. The funeral home wanted to start an autopsy, but I said, "I don't want to make any of these plans until we contact our son." Then we heard that he had been told and that he was coming home. He knew his brother was dead, but he didn't know any more, and telling him the circumstances was hard too. It tore me apart.

My husband had shut down. He tried to keep things going, but we each stayed by ourselves and dealt with it in our own way. He thought about putting a contract out on someone to kill Gregory. A couple of men came to the door soon after the incident and said, "Look, for this much money we can arrange for him to be killed."

But I said to my husband, "Jim, two wrongs don't make a right. Let it go. God will take care of it. Let the courts handle him." I still had enough faith in me, at that stage, to keep him from doing wrong. So he dropped the whole idea.

He started drinking quite a lot in the bar on the way home from work, though, and we might well have ended up divorced. We were living with my mother, and he came home several times drunk. I could only say, "Jim, please don't do this to me. I need you; I need your help." After a while I asked, "Would you do me a favor?"

And he said, "What?"

I said, "I'm not going to ask you to give up your drinking, but what I'm asking you to do for me is go to therapy with me."

He agreed to come to therapy and often he would come drunk. In the end, about 1985, I had just had enough. I couldn't take the pain anymore, and I was going to get a lawyer and file for a divorce. When I told my therapist, she said, "Hold on, hold on. Let me work at this." So she got a friend and they sat Jim down and told him. He knew he had a problem and agreed to go into rehab. He went there for 30 days and he hasn't had anything to drink since. After he sobered up, he was altogether different.

In the meantime, Gregory was charged with murder. He was 16 and still in the juvenile system, so everything about him was kept very hushed up. We didn't know anything for two years. When he left our house, he was taken in the ambulance to a hospital in the University of Maryland, where he survived and had a prosthesis put in his jaw.

It was two years before I discovered that Gregory had been on drugs that night. He bought some drugs—marijuana, PCP—with his birthday money and took them to the party. Tony had drunk some beer but did not take any drugs. I always knew that Greg would have had to flip out to commit a heinous crime like that. Something was clearly wrong for him to do something like that. For all this time, I wanted him to suffer and to live with his mistake for the rest of his life. I didn't actually hate him because I still had that love in me for him, but my anger was intense. I just wanted him to be accountable for his mistakes and be punished. When the state's attorney asked me and my husband, "Do you want him to have the death penalty?" my husband and I looked at each other and I said, "Well, I don't.'"

And he said "Well, I don't either." He added, "We just want him to be punished."

In the end, he was sentenced to 25 years imprisonment, with the possibility of probation at some later stage. After that, we took the State of Baltimore County to court in a separate court case because they were in charge of the juvenile system, and they never told us that Greg had a drug background. Our argument was that if, as foster parents, we had been informed of his drug history, we could have prevented having our son murdered. We ended up winning the case and receiving fifty thousand dollars, but it all left us with nothing but emptiness. It caused us to lose faith in a lot of things, even God.

For about two or three years, I stopped going to church altogether. It was like living in a dark tunnel that had no light. It was so depressing. My sisters, Anne and Jean, stopped going too—and my sister Elaine only went to take my mother along each Sunday. We felt so distant from God and we were all going through therapy.

After a few years, I drifted back to church occasionally, but I couldn't talk to God. I felt estranged from Him. Instead of praying, I would sit in church and just talk to my son, Tony. I couldn't even say the "Our Father" because it stuck in my throat. I felt God had let me down and betrayed me. I only went to church at all because of a kind of sense of duty. I thought I might otherwise be condemned to hell forever.

In 1996, Greg had served 12 years in prison, and he was released. I wrote letters and asked them to keep him in longer, but they said that he had gone through the system and passed with flying colors and would be released.

One day in 1997, I read about a "healing service" at the church, St. Clare's Catholic Church, which was coming up the following week. I was very depressed, and I remember saying to myself, "I can't live this way anymore. I've got to go."

So I went to the healing service, and there were lay ministers there sitting in chairs who said, "If you have any kind of health problem and you want to be healed, come and ask one of us to pray for you." I looked around and I didn't really trust anybody there. Then I saw a man who I knew vaguely from church, and I went over to him. He looked at me and said, "How can I pray for you? What is it you want?"

And I said, "I want healing."

As I sat on a chair, he started praying over me. He laid his hands on my head, and at once, I felt this immense energy that came through me. It was like a beacon of light shining through my whole being. Suddenly I found myself crying and crying. It was so emotional. Then I raised my arms to God and said a prayer out loud, "Forgive me, my Lord. Take me into your heart and forgive me for what I have done." I kept saying, "Please forgive me, please forgive me." And as I sat there, God just came into my soul to forgive me and to give me light and no more darkness. I could feel the power going through my hands and down my arms and into my whole being.

After that, I started going regularly to church on Sundays, and it was then that I noticed an advertisement for this course called Alpha in the church bulletin. It said it was an introduction to Christianity, and I said to myself, "Well, I'll give it a shot. What the heck?"

It was held on a Tuesday evening, and I guess there were maybe 35 to 40 people there. I walked in expecting that it would be quite intense, but I just felt myself surrounded by all this love. As soon as I arrived, the Alpha team leader, Vicky, came up to me and said, "Welcome." I enjoyed the evening and went back the following week. After that session, I said to myself, "Gee, this is pretty good. I'm getting better; I'm feeling better." Everyone was just so friendly.

As the course went on, the more everything made sense to me. At my Catholic school they used to teach Bible scriptures and stuff like that, but I never really understood why God did what He did. I knew that we had a Bible but reading the Gospels and the Epistles every Sunday was as far as we got. Now I was getting involved deeper and deeper in the Bible—and reading it by myself.

The other significant thing was that there was a session which covered the importance of forgiveness. I felt God saying that I needed to forgive Greg if I was to receive everything that God wanted to give me. This was something that worked on my mind for weeks and months, days and nights, until finally I said to myself, "I have to do this." So I forgave Greg in my heart, and then prayed to God to forgive me for holding that hatred of Greg for so long. It was a very big thing for me to do, but I felt so much better afterward.

When the Alpha course ended, I said to my sisters, "This is an amazing course. You must come with me to the next

next one." Then, in the middle of 1998, our mother was taken very ill with cancer and was hospitalized. Anne, Jean, and I were in the waiting room at the hospital when we saw an ambulance driver walk through the room to pick up a patient to take him home. I looked at the man and recognized him. He had a big beard to cover his scars, but I recognized his eyes. I turned to my sisters and said, "I think I saw Greg." I hadn't seen him since the day of the murder.

Anne said, "Are you sure?"

Then Jean said to Anne, "I'm going to find out if that was Greg.'"

She said, "Go ahead, Jean."

So Jean went and found the man and said, "Excuse me, but you look awfully familiar. Would your name be Greg?"

And he said, "Yes."

"What's your last name?"

"Bryer."

And she said, "Well, thank you," and she turned on her heels and walked straight back to our waiting room. She said, "You are right, Marge. You're right."

At that, Anne said, "Let me at him!" She was ready to tear him apart, but we held her back and blocked the doorway. She said, "How can you be so calm?"

And I replied, "I have forgiven him. I have not forgotten what he has done, but I have had to forgive him."

At that, she got very angry with me and said, "I can't believe you said that." In the end she just walked away. She couldn't deal with it.

We didn't see Greg again after that. He clearly knew

who we were, and he decided to keep away. Soon afterward, our mother died of cancer. Elaine was very interested in taking an Alpha course, so we did the course together—and she became closer and closer to Jesus as the course went on. At the end of the course, the two of us held each other and prayed to the Lord and said, "Now we have to work on our other sisters." We prayed and told God how desperately we wanted to get our other sisters, Anne and Jean, into the faith. We knew that God was alive.

Meanwhile, Anne had seen the change in Elaine and me and particularly noticed how we so often had smiles on our faces. She thought, *How can they be so happy?* And I kept saying to her, "Anne, I've found my faith. Why don't you come to an Alpha course?" To start with, she said no, but then in February of 2000, she agreed.

On the first night, she arrived too late for the meal and then sat in the back row. But she kept coming back and clearly enjoyed it more and more. Then, on the weekend retreat, she went up for prayer and as they prayed for her, she cried and cried. It was clearly the Holy Spirit because she kept on talking about it, saying, "This feeling is so new to me. I'm just so happy. I don't feel all that guilt anymore." And she gave her life to Jesus that day. Some time afterward, she forgave Greg herself, and we all started praying for him. We haven't seen him since that day in the hospital, but we pray for him.

Now we are all three involved with ministry at St. Clare's, and our lives have changed around completely. For me, I feel that my total healing came the day I forgave

Greg. I completely came out of my shell that day, and things have been different ever since. Suddenly, I wasn't in that dark tunnel anymore.

Jesus used to be so distant from me, but now He is my whole being. He makes it worth opening my eyes in the morning.

Marjorie Foor still attends St. Clare's Catholic Church, where she is now a "Eucharist minister" and a team member on their Alpha course. She says, "God has guided my life every step of the way."

"I didn't care who I ran over. If people got in my way, that was too bad for them."

2

THE STORY OF DAN COURTRIGHT

At the age of 21, Dan Courtright became a biker traveling around the U.S. with no helmet, no I.D., and taking part in regular gang fights which the police would watch from a safe distance—even when those involved were killed or maimed. Then, in September of 2000, he saw an advertisement for a church course which said, "If you have questions about Christianity, come and join us."

My dad was in the army and my mom was in the State Department, so during my childhood we traveled all over the world. At various times, we lived in Germany, France, Greece, Spain, and England as well as the U.S.. In

1968, my older brother, David, was killed while serving in Vietnam with the military. He was 18 and my mom and dad didn't take it too well. A year later, when I was about ten, they got divorced and I stayed with my mom. We continued to travel a lot. I had another brother, and we treated the break-up of our parents' marriage as pretty normal. A stable family isn't something that's common in either military or diplomatic life.

I started drinking at age 12 or 13 and was soon drinking a gallon of beer on party nights—sometimes a gallon and a half. I would also drink wine. By 1977, when I was 18, we were living in Israel just north of Tel Aviv. I graduated from the American International school there. At that time, I could speak four languages—English, French, German, and Hebrew.

After graduation, I joined the Air Force, but three years later I got out of that and went to Boston, where I started work on a degree in engineering. It was there that I learned that I had a son, Daniel—born to the girlfriend I left when I walked out of the Air Force. After getting my degree, I started traveling around the country—constantly on the move. No matter where I went I'd just find a place, live and work for a while, and then go somewhere else when I got tired of it. My brother lived with his wife and children—he's the stable one—and I would check back with them every couple of years. They were always around, and if I needed somewhere to go, I could always crash at their house.

I got my first bike, a Kawasaki KZ450, when I was 25—

about 1985. It was a bit of a basket case which I put together myself. That was how I got into the biking world. I enjoyed it immediately; you've got your drugs, your women—whatever you want. It's kind of like the gangs in L.A. or anywhere else, where you've got your colors that you fly, and everybody knows who you are.

I became known as "Hoss" because my last name is Courtright. Everybody thinks "Cart-right." I'm a pretty good sized guy, so Hoss fit. Plus I'm pretty friendly usually—just don't get me mad! There are the bars that you hang out at, and as long as the cops aren't around, you can do anything that you want. And even if they are, it really doesn't matter. If you were in a cop car cruising by and saw a couple of guys doing something illegal—but with ten more guys with nothing to lose hanging around—what would you do? If you're a cop with a family, you don't want to walk over and say, "Hi, you're busted," when those other guys may say, "No pal, you're busted. We'll bust you up." When you've got nothing to lose, what does it matter to guys like that? Have you ever not had to answer to any-body—done what you wanted to do when you wanted to do it?

As a biker, you basically just got to be a kid and do what you wanted. All right, there were certain unofficial rules you had to follow. There's things you don't talk about, and there's things you don't do. You don't take somebody else's stash. You don't try to rip your own brother. If you do things like that, you'd best just leave and don't bother to come back, because if you get a bad rep, sooner or later something's going to catch up with you. Word travels down the line.

At one time, I worked for the "carny"—the carnival—that set up in places and had fairs, with rides and things like that. That was pretty rough, with a lot of underground stuff. Everybody knows you don't mess with the carny because if you do, you are going to get hurt. Sometimes, I got cut up [knifed] because if I don't like someone I'm going to say so, and I'm going to do something about it. There were a lot of knives around. I was probably involved in fights about three or four times a week. There's a lot of things you don't hear about on the news. People disappear, and you never hear about it because they probably didn't have any official I.D. anyway. I had no official I.D. for quite a few years.

As time went on, I was drinking a lot. One rule I had with myself, though, was that I would never drink when I was working. I may go in a little drunk—that's a different story—but I'd never drink while I was working. If I was off work, though, I might wake in the morning and drink a bottle of scotch.

I've nearly died a few times. In 1998 in Tulsa, I was on my bike in the wrong area and without any friends. There were more of them than there was of me, and I got cut up and left for dead. I got stabbed through the ribs on my left side just under the heart. The blade went in about six inches and just nicked the heart, though it didn't puncture the lungs. That was my closest call. I've had some other near misses. I've been cut in the head and various other places in my body—as well as being in some bike wrecks.

No helmets, of course. I mean, if you're going to go, you're going to go. If your head's going to hit a pole, the only difference if you've got a helmet is that you look prettier in a casket. If you're dead, you're dead. A lot of friends lost legs, arms, eyes. It was just a fact of life.

In gang wars, it's like "us against them." If somebody started messing with one of your brother's bikes or someone is messing with your buddy's old lady and they don't want nothing to do with it, it's kind of, "OK, pal, we've got a problem." We try to settle it by putting a couple of guys against a couple of guys, but you never know what leads to what. Things happen, old grudges take effect real quick, and it goes all out. Cops stay away from them too. They just let them deal with it. The cops' attitude is, "They're not hurting anybody else. Let them kill themselves."

There were usually not a lot of gun fights because once that happens you start hitting the bigger league where cops get called in, and the FBI gets called in. You want to avoid that kind of attention. My brother is a cop, so I had to be real nice when I was around him. I'd get a lot of lectures, but he's a pretty good guy and wouldn't say much. Nevertheless, I had to be real cool at his place, because all of his friends were cops. I was on good behavior because that was his turf.

In 1995, I met a lady in the carny world, and after a couple of years traveling together she became pregnant. She had family in Missouri, and we went to Tulsa. I got a job and played the good guy for a while. She had our daughter, Danielle Marie, on August 16, 1997, and after about a year

I wanted to travel again. I was just getting itchy. So she went to her dad's and that was the last time I saw my daughter. I went back into my lifestyle again, forgot about being nice, and so we both thought it would be best if I didn't come around.

Around that time, I saw my son, Dan, for the first time. It was a 20-minute meeting in a controlled environment with my brother and his grandparents present. They wanted to make sure nothing went on and got said. He was about 18 years old. For him, I suppose it was a bit like seeing an uncle you've never met before. For me, it was like, "OK, this is my son." It was very formal, and there was no real emotion there at all.

I did drugs—stuff like crank and crystal—recreationally, but alcohol was my thing. I was drinking half a gallon of whisky a night and still getting up and going to work the next morning. To me, that is excessive. I had seen the inside of quite a few jails because of my drinking. If I sat down and stopped drinking for a day, next day I'd start shaking and by that night I wouldn't be able to grab hold of a glass. So I just kept drinking. It stopped me from shaking and still felt good. I was addicted.

One day in May of 2000, I was staying in a motel in Cleveland, Oklahoma, and I got tired of it all. I was lying on the bed watching TV and I said, "This ain't right." Then I got off the bed, stood up, and asked God to help me quit drinking. I believed there was a God out there, but I didn't really know a whole lot. I'd seen the evangelists on TV going, "I'll save your soul—just send me twenty-five dollars." It was like, "Come on, give me a break." I decided to stop drinking, and the next morning I quit my job. By that evening, I was shaking like a leaf. I spent about three days going through hell.

It took me about three days before I could do anything. I couldn't eat because I couldn't hold on to anything with my hands. On the fifth or sixth day, I said to my buddy, "Can you circle around Tulsa? I need to go into rehab." I knew I was thinking about starting to drink again.

On May 25, 2000, I went into a Salvation Army rehab, and I started to do the 12-step program. I worked hard to keep my mind from straying, and in August or September I was invited to a local church, the First United Methodist Church in Tulsa, by Richard, a friend from rehab.

I went to the church the following Sunday, and I saw an advertisement for an Alpha class starting that Tuesday. The advertisement said, "If you have questions about Christianity, come and join us." So I decided to check out what was going on.

I didn't know what to expect, but the first night I turned up and found it was being held in a church room with about 12 people. I was as nervous as a long-tailed cat in a room full of rocking chairs. I just sat back in the corner and watched what was going on. We had a little supper and played a "name game." I called myself Daring Dan, which I thought was appropriate. The people were real nice, and I told them a little bit about myself and that I'd just come "to check this out." We watched the video, and I kind of enjoyed the group, so I came back the next Tuesday.

Nevertheless, walking into the church I was scared thumbless, waiting for the roof to fall in.

I had always felt that there was a God, but I really didn't know much about God or Jesus or anything like that. In the group, I was the one that said, "Listen, I'm going to ask a lot of stupid questions." Once, during the second or third session, I asked one particular question of Stephanie, one of the leaders, and she just said, "I don't know," which I thought was great. I think that's when I relaxed and thought, *OK, I'm in the right place.*

All my life, I had felt that the minister guy up at the front of the church was kind of unapproachable. You don't like to bother him with stupid questions because he's got church things to do. But at Alpha I could start asking those stupid little questions, and I started feeling at ease. We did the Alpha weekend at the church and that was good. And as the weeks went on, I decided to become a Christian.

At the time, I was still living in the rehab and was doing maintenance work with the Salvation Army there. I'd been off drink and drugs since May 2000, but it would have been easy to go back.

My attitude toward Jesus was that He was up there on the cross and got crucified. The way I looked at it was that He was a stupid idiot who probably shouldn't have been at the place He'd gotten to. He'd gone too far. Man, even with our government if you talk too loud, you aren't going to be around too long. That's just the facts of life. That's the way I looked at it. But during the course I realized that He had died on the cross for our sins. He died because of the things

I'd done before He even knew me.

I decided to let Jesus into my life, and still it is emotional to me. I feel Him in my heart knowing that I can do good because He did good. I know I'm doing the right thing. I also know I'm now doing some things God's way instead of my way. I just pray and let God direct me where I'm going. Jesus was the one who opened those doors.

Before, I didn't care who I ran over. If people got in my way, that was too bad for them. I also knew that if I got in their way, that was too bad for me. But now I try to look ahead and think, *OK, what does God want me to do? How do I need to do things?* I'm trying to do things according to His will. I'm just looking at things from a different perspective than what I used to. Jesus says to love one another, and I'm trying to see how that fits together with what I do.

Now, almost every morning, when I go and do my thing in the bathroom, I'll look in the mirror, and I'll ask Jesus to come walk with me. I say, "Just take a walk with me, Bud." I do it in my own language. If I want Jesus to be my buddy, I'm going to talk to Him the way I want to talk to Him. So I say something like, "OK, Bud, come on. I'm heading on out. Why don't you come on a walk with me today?" And during the day I just try to talk to Him. I used to read the Bible at times, but now when I read it, I am trying to understand it. Now I read a bit and say to myself, "What the heck does this mean?"

Now, on Sundays, I go to the Salvation Army Church where I live and then, when that service is over, I go straight to First United Methodist Church. Sometimes I won't make either one, but I'm going to church a lot more regularly than I used to. I'm a changed person—I know that—and the more that I'm learning about Jesus, I think I'm becoming a better person. And in becoming a better person, maybe I can help other people to become better people also.

I've got an I.D. now. I don't have any credit, but I'm starting to establish an identity again. I lost my driver's license about five years ago—at least, they nullified it—but now I've just gotten it back. I'm no longer going to go to my old lifestyle. There's a lot of people I hurt because I really didn't care what anybody else thought. By having the attitude that you can do anything, you are going to hurt people. I'm not going to quit riding. It's just the places and the people I'm going to not associate with anymore. There's a lot I probably will see because they are basically good people, and they just don't know.

I've had a lot of friends say to me, "Hey, man, you know you've changed. You are the same person, but you've changed. You just don't do that anymore."

And I say, "Nah, man, I don't—and I'm comfortable with it."

Dan Courtright is currently in the choir of his local church, which he attends regularly. He has been a helper, a leader, and co-leader for Alpha. On May 17, 2002, he married Marjorie, whom he met during Alpha. He says, "I have Jesus to thank for all my blessings. Thank you, Lord."

*"Beatings were what I knew. That was what men did.
It's all I have ever seen all my life."*

THE STORY OF VERONICA

Born in a prison, the daughter of a prostitute, Veronica became a stripper, a drug addict, and served time in jail. It was while in a New Hampshire prison for violence in 2000 that some ladies at a local church gave her a video to watch. Here she describes how her life changed.

I was born on August 31, 1965, in Framington State Prison, a women's prison in Massachusetts. My mother was a prostitute who took drugs and was in for armed robbery. I don't know who my dad is. She had been let out of prison before I was born but had to go back for getting pregnant with me. That was a violation of her parole. She resented me partly because of that, I suppose.

After six months I went to live with my grandma, who had 15 children. She is a lovely woman, now in her eighties. After I went to live with her, I didn't see my mother for four years. We lived in a four-bedroom home, and soon after I arrived my grandfather left, so there was just my grandmother raising all of us. One of my uncles is six months older than me and another is a little bit younger.

When my mom got out of prison, she met a man, got married, and took me back to live with her. I was about six. I had a very abusive stepfather. He was an alcoholic and would beat the daylights out of us (mom and he had two other children). I was also sexually abused by my uncles. I probably started marijuana at age 10 or 11 and coke at 12 or 13.

I tried running away about 30 times but only succeeded when I was 14. The carnival was in town, and they were in need of help, so I joined up with them and left home for good. I was a young, pretty girl at the time and took the part of "Tiny Tricia," a little six-inch girl, in one of the side shows. There is a mirror which creates the illusion, but everyone paid a dollar to come in and see me. I was also very good at getting guys in to spend money on various games, like throwing a ball into goblets. If you could throw it into a blue goblet, you got a big prize—but there was only one blue goblet. Basically, we were ripping people off, and I did that for quite a few years.

The lifestyle of those in the carnival was terrible. It was all drugs—a huge drug lifestyle, cocaine, crack. By the time I was 15, I was shooting intravenously. Everyone gets up first thing in the morning, and you rarely go to bed until after two or three o'clock in the morning. That is a lot of work. We drove around from state to state in great big 18-wheelers.

As "Tiny Tricia" I was earning about fifteen hundred dollars a week at the age of 15, but I spent most of it on my severe drug habit. I used to use a lot of crank, which is something you sniff. Like cocaine, it keeps you awake, and at one point I had blisters all down my nose and my throat. I did a lot of degrading things over the years, posing in magazines and stripping and working in dance halls. I was never a prostitute, though, because I think I resented my mom for that.

I moved around with several different carnys. Once, I left the carnival for a little while and went to Florida and became a stripper. While there, I got arrested for disorderly conduct and drinking. I was in jail for 20 days: no big deal—you're there until you pay your fine off. I then returned to New Hampshire, got arrested for under-age drinking and went to jail for 19 days. I was 20 years old. By then, I was engaged to be married to a guy named Richard, who I had met while hanging out at a biker bar doing a lot of drugs. He was so sweet and good looking and looked like the boy next door.

We got married in 1986 after I'd got out of jail. I was 21 and thought I was getting out of my lifestyle with drugs. We were married at St. Matthew's Episcopal Church in Goffstown, but the wedding was a nightmare. Richard's parents absolutely hated me after discovering that I had once posed nude for a national magazine. They had begged me and begged me to let them do the catering for the 80 guests at the wedding. Richard's father worked at Notre Dame College, which had a culinary section, I guess.

Anyway, I thought they were going to hire somebody to do the catering, but on the day they showed up with 12 sandwiches cut into fours. I spent the whole morning crying. Me and the girls had to run to the grocery store, where we bought baloney and ham and turkey, rolled it up and made lunch for 80 in 45 minutes. That couple just hated me so much.

After four years of marriage, I found out that Richard was intravenously using cocaine. By then, I had finished with drugs and we had two children—Joshua, who was born in 1988, and Britney, who was born in 1990. I didn't know he was doing it, because he was a mechanic and he welded, so he had burn marks all over his arms. I only found out about it because somebody told me. I arranged for him to get into a rehab, which costs a lot of money, but he walked out two days later. When he did that, I just had it. I couldn't do it anymore, so I took the kids to an apartment and started all over again. I was too weak. With two little babies, I couldn't be using drugs. What if we both died? If we both died of an overdose, who was going to take care of my kids? Richard is now in federal prison in Fort Dix, New Jersey.

Soon after leaving Richard, I started going out with Daryl, who is African American, and father of my son Jacob, who was born on October 18, 1994. Daryl was also into drugs and was very abusive. I had to stay home all the time with the kids, and if I complained, he came home and beat me. I moved in and out, in and out, in and out.

Beatings to me was what I knew. That was what men did.

They beat their wives. It's all I have ever seen all my life. By the time Jacob was born, I had gone back to college where I got my associate's degree in paralegal. Jacob was born right before I graduated. Soon after that, I stood up to Daryl for the first time, and he beat me in front of my daughter. I couldn't take it anymore, and I called the police and had him arrested.

Then I was alone with my children for two years and we were happy. We started going to a little Baptist church in Manchester, New Hampshire, and I got a good job working as a legal administrator in a very large collection agency. I moved up very quickly and ended up being Director of Employee Development in less than two years. Unfortunately, while there I met some friends who were into the drug scene and, through them, I got into crack. I tried it for the first time in 1997 and became addicted. Crack is terrible. I don't know why it is so addictive, because only the first hit is any good and the rest of it stinks—but you chase the high.

At that time, I met Brian, who was also addicted to crack. He settled in with me and the three children and, with us both very much into drugs, that whole first year was really fuzzy. I don't know what kind of a mother I was. I have no idea. I was completely and totally addicted to drugs. In 1998, we moved up to Newport and rented a house. Though I was still doing drugs, I started going to church because I wanted something for the kids. I took them every Sunday. Brian and I married in 1999.

Then came an incident which resulted in me going to

jail. Since Jacob is "mulatto" (half black), some children would call him names. Usually, when I went to speak to the parents about it, they were very nice. On this occasion, I went to the parents' house and this woman said, "So he is a nigger and you're a nigger loving whore." At that, I lost it and beat the heck out of her. Then the cops came and I beat up the cops. I have a very violent background. I lived on the streets with the carnival, and you learn to fight. I got a year in jail, but because the church wrote a letter for me, in the end, the court gave me all but 60 days suspended. So on January 4, 2000, I went to jail for 60 days.

The ladies in my church (there are about ten of them—all over 60) knew nothing of my background, so I had to come clean and tell them that I was going to jail. I was going to jail on a Monday morning and the day before—Sunday—I went to church and told them. I waited until the last minute, because I didn't want them to hate me and wanted them to like my children. But they were lovely about it and one of them, a lady called Flora Kangis, came and prayed over me. She prayed in tongues, and a great feeling of peace came over me. I had never heard anybody do that before.

Flora is the sweetest, dearest lady. She is 72 or 73 and an incredible woman of faith. She visited me in jail every week with her sister, never missed. They came up and we did Bible study. Meanwhile, the church people were wonderful to my children. Even though my husband is a complete atheist, they kept dropping off casseroles and other food for him and the children. They were so nice to him.

They had started running the Alpha course at the church, and the ladies gave me the first video, with three talks on it, and a copy of the book *Questions of Life*. After they had gone, I sat down and watched them at one sitting all by myself. After watching the video, I read the book from cover to cover.

When I came out of jail, I started doing the course with them each week. I missed the weekend away because I didn't have the money to go on it, but the ladies gave me the video, and I watched it with my kids at home. As I sat watching, all of a sudden I realized I was crying. Josh and Britney were watching it with me. I've done a lot of things in my life that I have always been ashamed of. Nicky [Nicky Gumbel, the Alpha course speaker] suggested saying a prayer accepting Jesus as my Lord and Savior, but before that, he suggested that I think of everything that I had done wrong. That took a long time; it seemed like forever. I had to get rid of all that badness that I had been carrying around all these years, all the guilt. It was like everything that I had ever done came into my head, and I said, "Forgive me for this." Then I felt clean enough that I could ask Jesus to come into my heart.

Now I know God loves me, and He wants me to do something. I don't know what He wants me to do yet, but I know that He wants me to do something. The Christian life is pretty simple. Just love each other and love God—that's all we really have to do. Life is pretty simple once you let go of all the bad parts. There's only one Person who can carry all that dirty laundry.

Not long ago, I was always fighting, always getting into drugs. I was nasty. I was mean. I was the bully. I beat people up because I was poor and they had better clothes than me, or better hair than me. But now I am clean of drugs.

Now Jesus is my best friend. I used to get up and say to God, "Why are you putting me through this?" But now, every day I get up and thank Him for my blessings.

Veronica is now running a youth group at her church. She has asked that her last name not be revealed to allow her to grow in her new life in the church.

3

THE STORY OF JAMIE FURNEY

Jamie Furney, of Albuquerque, New Mexico, was furious when her local Episcopal bishop made comments about her homosexual lifestyle. But an extraordinary change in his attitude a year later made her think again about Christianity.

When I was nine years old, my father committed suicide. I don't really know why, but he fought in Vietnam and was never very stable. I don't think he and my mother got along, either. My dad and I always had things in common, while my mom and my sister were always more alike. So when dad died, I sat around thinking, *Where do I fit?* By the time I graduated from high school, I left. I went to Dallas, Texas, because I wanted to get as far away from home as I could. I just said, "Oh, I'll get a job and just live my life," which I did. I didn't really blame God. I wasn't even sure if He was there. Neither my mom or dad went to church. I went with friends from school to the local Episcopal church from time to time, but only because they were going.

In Dallas I worked for about four years, up to 1990, as a collector for a company which collected bad debts. During that time, I did a lot of drinking and carrying on and having all kinds of fun with my friends. I started living a homosexual lifestyle—something I had been doing off and on since I was 15—and would attend "Gay Pride" days and things like that, though I didn't participate in them. I would just kind of watch.

When I look back on it, my drinking was excessive. I wouldn't classify myself as an alcoholic. I was just young and stupid and thought I could live through anything. I would get drunk two or three nights a week.

During my time in Dallas, members of my family had started to attend church. In 1986, my sister, Kellie, had planned to get married in the Episcopal church I used to attend as a child, because it is a real old Hispanic-style building and she loved it. To make sure she and her fiancé could marry there, they attended services for six months beforehand. Then the engagement ended, but my sister continued attending the church. I had felt she was a real hypocrite to go to the church simply because she wanted to be married there. My mother had also started going, so whenever I came home to visit, we would go to church. I thought, *OK. There's worse things they could do, I suppose.* It didn't mean anything to me.

Then, on the Saturday before Easter 1986, we went to church; I can't remember why. During the service, my mother, who was sitting in the front pew, started crying. I think she cried for three or four hours. I couldn't believe what was going on. I was like, *What is wrong with her? What has happened to my mother? She's nuts. Somebody bring my mother back.* Long after the service ended, she was still there, and in the end I left her there crying.

That was the beginning of a new Christian life for her, and she's been a rock-solid Christian ever since. But as for me, I wasn't interested in it. It was just, *OK, she goes to church. That's all I need to know.* She did change after that day, though. She had never been a particularly happy person—particularly after my father died, when she didn't set foot outside the house for four years. But now she was happy. She seemed to be a softer person. She seemed to be kinder. She would call me up in Dallas and say, "How are you doing?" and "I just wanted to let you know I love you." That was something that had never happened before. Before that Saturday, I would call once every two or three months to tell her I was still alive. That was it.

In 1990, my sister and brother-in-law moved to Holland because of his work, and my mother, who was not really young then, called me and said, "You know I'm here all by myself. I really wish you'd come back. You could find a job out here close to the one you have." I thought about it and, just to make her happy, applied for a job in New Mexico that was similar to the work I'd been doing in Dallas. I got the job and, after more thought, said, "OK, I'll do it." So I ended up going home to Clovis to live with my mother. I still didn't go to church, except at Christmas and Easter.

In 1991, my work moved me to Albuquerque, three hours away, and I took the job because it meant more money. By then I was working more and more. I had given up on life as it was and decided just to work. I thought, If I work really hard I won't have time *to go out drinking and keep being stupid, so I'll just work.* And that's what I did. I worked 15– to 16-hour days, every day, seven days a week. I didn't care. And I moved up pretty rapidly in the company, because I was so devoted to my work.

In 1993, I grew close to another woman and we moved in together. Up to then, I had been living alone. Some years later, a group at my mother's church started running a course called Alpha. My mom would tell me about how it was an introduction to Christianity, and I said, "Yeah, that sounds really neat." But I didn't really want to hear about it. Some time around 1996, I started attending a church in Albuquerque pretty regularly. But nobody ever spoke to me when I went—for two years. After that I decided I hated church. I said, "Why am I here? Two years and nobody said a word!"

In 1998, my mother invited me and my sister and brother-in-law (who had by now returned from living in Holland) to a church event called "Summer Harvest," which is the diocese annual "family gathering." While we were there, the Bishop of the Diocese of the Rio Grande, Terence Kelshaw, spoke, and one of his main topics was homosexuality. It just sounded like hell-fire and brimstone to me. He basically said, "Gays are going to go to hell if they don't change their lives. And I'm not going to be the kind of bishop that stands up here and claims to justify it in any way. If it's wrong, it's wrong, and everybody knows it's wrong. So that's it." The more he spoke, the more I thought, *What's the point of even trying? You're not ever going to get there.* I got really irritated by it, and the more I sat there and listened, the madder I got. So I went up to him afterward and said, "What if you're wrong? What if everything you're saying up there is not true? What if God loves me right where I am today?"

We argued back and forth, and he pulled out Bible verses and theology and said, "Well, this is why I'm right."

And I said, "Well, it doesn't do anything for me. If God's not going to love me the way I am right this moment, then I don't really need Him."

He said, "You can't do that. God doesn't want you to live that way."

I said, "If I want to live in a homosexual relationship, how can you tell me I'm wrong? What if I'm right? I might be right. You might be wrong. And when we all get there, what are we going to do?"

Well, he didn't have a whole lot of answers, and I thought, *Whatever. I'm not going to talk to this man any-more.* And I left. His attitude was very different from that of my mother's group of Christian friends. They all knew about my lifestyle, and not one of them ever judged me. They all just loved me. I thought that was the way to be rather than standing up in the pulpit like the Bishop saying, "You're going to hell and that's the end of it."

At the end of 1998, the Bishop and his wife went away on sabbatical and attended an Alpha conference [a conference to train church leaders in how to run the Alpha course] in Singapore. In February of 1999, he returned, and my mother and her friends were due to see him again at the annual Women's Retreat for the diocese at which he was speaking. They said, "You should come with us."

I said, "You guys are nuts. I'm not going with you."

They told me, "You've got to go. He's different. There's something different about him, and you're going to like what he has to say. You really need to go."

In the end they managed to talk me into going to dinner there on that Friday night. I said, "Whatever happens, I'm not talking to that man. I am not talking to him."

The dinner party went well, and then my mother's friends invited me to their Saturday lunch the next day. And because I liked these people, I said, "Yeah, I'll go and have lunch with you." Afterward, they persuaded me to go to listen to the next session of the retreat. They said, "Look, you know we love you. You know we wouldn't do anything to hurt you. We really want you to come listen." So I finally had to give in because they were right. I knew they loved me. And when I listened to the Bishop, I couldn't believe what he was saying. He said, "It's not our place to judge people. It's our place to love them. That's all we're called to do—just love people." I was stunned. And my mom's friends were all sitting there watching me to see if I noticed that there was a difference. And sure enough, I noticed. At the end, I said, "Yeah, there's a difference."

I still didn't want to talk to the Bishop afterward, so I started walking out the door when he grabbed my arm. He said, "Things are different, aren't they?"

And I said, "Yeah. They are."

Then he said he was sorry for the way he had spoken to me before. I couldn't believe it. It was amazing. Finally, he asked me if I would do something for him. He said, "I want you to go to this church—Trinity Episcopal Church in Albuquerque." And he gave me the address. He said, "I want you to get involved in the Alpha program. Check it out and let me know what you think."

He was so polite that I said, "Well, I can do that for you."

It was the course my mom had mentioned, which I thought was interesting. I went to the first meeting and sat there and thought, *Well, it's OK*. They all wanted to know why I was there, and I said, "My mother and the Bishop told me to check it out, so here I am." There were about 40 or 50 people there, and I never missed a night.

It was quite weird because at this stage everything else in my life was falling apart. The relationship that I had been in for six years was falling apart, I was starting to hate my job, and I had had pneumonia twice in three months. It was a really emotional time. Alpha on Sunday nights was the highlight during this destruction that was going on in my life. The course's weekend away was May 23 and I will never forget it. I didn't want to go, but there was this other young girl on the course who didn't have a car, and I had agreed to give her a ride. The place we were going was about an hour and a half away.

On the Saturday, we watched the talks on video and, after the one in the afternoon, the leader invited the Holy Spirit to come. At that, this friend, Cindy, asked if she could pray for me. As she prayed, we were singing a song called, "I will change your name." I don't remember the words exactly but they were something like, "I Will Change Your Name. You will no longer be called lonely, outcast, or afraid. Your new name will be friend of God, one who seeks my face." At that I started to cry like you wouldn't believe. I just couldn't stop. And as I sat there, I thought, *I'm going to test this. I know I'm not supposed to test God, but I'm going to.* So, in my own head, I said to God, "If this is real, if I'm not losing my mind, I want to see what You look like. I can't believe in something I can't see." And at that moment, right in front of my face, there was Jesus.

And I went, "Wow." I said, "You're real."

And He said, "Yes. And I can change your name," (like in the song which was being sung).

I said, "OK."

He said, "Don't take your eyes off Me. Just keep your eyes on Me and everything will be fine."

I then said, "I'll give You my life. I'll do anything You want me to. I'll follow You and do whatever You say."

Then all of a sudden, I stopped crying. I couldn't stop

smiling. I smiled for two weeks. When I got home, I instantly knew that the way I'd been living my life was wrong. I wanted no part of it anymore. I couldn't do it. So I went to the person that I'd been living with since 1993 and said, "I can't do this anymore. I can't." I told her about my new faith in Jesus and said, "He's got something for me to do, and I don't have time for this. I need to follow what Jesus wants." It was hard, but our relationship had not been very easy recently anyway, so that made it a bit easier.

Jesus is everything to me now, and I can only say that the clouds look whiter, the grass looks greener, jokes are funnier, food tastes better . . . . Everything in life is better.

In May of 2000, I went to my doctor for a physical and she said, "Your smoking is getting really bad. You need to quit."

I had been smoking for 20 years, since I was 16. I had tried to stop before and failed miserably, but I said, "OK, I'll quit."

She said she was going to put me on some medication to try to help me quit. She said, "I want you to take it for about a week. Pick a date somewhere in that week that you want to quit."

So I got out of the doctor's and said to myself, "Seven days from today, that's when I'm going to quit—and that'll be it." I looked at the calendar and saw that the day was May 23, 2000, exactly a year after that Alpha weekend. I went, "Oh my! This is real, I'm really going to quit this time!" And I did. I haven't smoked since.

I read the Bible every day now. If I'm looking for an

answer to a question or a problem now, I find the answer is there again and again. And I can read the Scripture like ten times, but when I need an answer it's like, "Oh, that's what that means." It's like you don't understand it until you can apply it to your life.

I don't remember my life before May 23, 1999. It's almost as if it never existed. I've tried to remember it, and I really can't. Jesus meant nothing to me before then, and now He is just life for me.

Jamie Furney remains a regular churchgoer and now works with Bishop Terence Kelshaw on a ministry for evangelism in New Mexico and Texas.

"We both had so many problems . . . our children were unruly and would skip school."

4

THE STORY OF DOUGLAS AND AUTUMN RIFFLE

In 1999, Douglas and Autumn Riffle became desperate. With six children to care for, their lives were increasingly dominated by alcohol and fighting. That was when Douglas issued an ultimatum to his wife: "Let's go to church."

DOUGLAS' STORY

I got involved in drugs from about the age of 14 or 15, and my nickname at high school was "Drug" instead of

Doug. I did hallucinogens, downers, pot, cocaine—everything except the needle. I also dealt a bit and, though I was never arrested or anything like that, I put my mother through living hell. I remember at the age of 15 or 16 I had a party at home. I had about two or three pounds of dope on a table, weighing it to sell, and half the school up partying. Someone called my mother at work, and she had to come home with the police and run everybody out. There were drugs and kegs of beer all over the place.

I left school and graduated early with a very good grade average despite my drug abuse. At the age of 18, I wanted to go off traveling from our home in Ohio to Texas with some friends. I was going to take my girlfriend with me, but her parents said, "The only way you can take her is to marry her."

I told her I would have to go by myself, but she said, "Oh, please don't leave me; please don't leave me. Let's go and get married. Mom and dad will pay for everything." So we got married, even though I felt kind of pushed into it. It was in a church because that was what her mother wanted. In the end, it was more or less her parents' wedding. They provided everything and did everything. That was 1976.

I had a drinking problem and was a drug user. My wife was also a drug user but not so bad. We went immediately to Texas and Arizona for a year before coming back to Ohio. We had a son the first year and another son two years later. Unfortunately, our marriage broke up after three years and we got divorced. The children stayed with their mother. I became real angry at myself and everybody around me because my life was so out of control. I had a real emptiness inside me.

One day I pulled my van off the side of the road and called my doctor. I knew that if I didn't do something about the anger building up in me that I was going to hurt myself or somebody else. I went to see him and found he had called in three psychologists. After they had spoken to me, they checked me straight into a psychiatric ward at a hospital. The first thing they wanted to do was give me drugs and I said, "I'm trying to get off them, man. I don't want them." I was kept in a room by myself, and whenever the psychiatrists came to talk to me, I said I wanted to be left alone. I wanted some peace.

One day I got really mad in my hospital room and kicked the dresser over. I then picked it up and smashed it against the wall. I heard the security guards coming, and I thought, *Oh, God, they're going to get me now.* I went to pick the chest up and noticed a Gideon Bible had fallen onto the floor. The guards then came in and threatened to put a straightjacket on me. After that I started reading the Bible and really searching. I asked God to give me a new life and new direction. Soon after, I felt I was ready to leave hospital. They tried to stop me, saying, "You can't leave; you can't leave."

I said, "I came in here on my own, so I'm walking out on my own."

I was in there for about 30 days. My life went back to being like it had been before. I went back to my ex-wife and the children, and in 1981 we decided to get married again. Things didn't go well, and after two years, my wife was back on the drugs and alcohol and I was drinking as well. After a couple of years, I decided I had had enough and in 1985 we got divorced again. This time I managed to gain custody of the children. At that stage I was trying to clean up my life, and I started going to church. That lasted for about a year. One day I spoke to the pastor about some personal things, and he preached about it at church. He didn't use my name, but he started preaching in a judgmental way, and I thought, *Wow—I'm out of here. If this is what church is about I don't want it.* And I left. I was very hurt and very angry.

In 1991, I went to a party and met someone called Autumn. She had recently been divorced and had started drinking heavily—and we got along real well. We started dating and drinking together, and we did a good job of it too. Autumn would drink beer at night until she passed out. She had been divorced twice and had three children from her first marriage, Allison, April, and Amy. In 1992, we had a daughter between us called Alivia.

We both had so many problems, that as a result, our children were unruly and would skip school and that sort of thing. We gave them no foundation. We didn't start living together until Alivia was about a year old. We then broke up in 1994, though we still saw each other the whole time and partied together. In 1998 we got back together.

Soon after that Autumn lost her mother and her younger brother died of cancer at age 39. She started drinking even more to hide the pain; she would drink heavily about three or four times a week late into the night and pass out. Then, after just two hours sleep, she would get up and go to work. She had a job working in finance for a large company, and I have no idea how she managed to function. She was like that until the end of 1998 when I said, "That's it—enough! I'm leaving. I can't take this any more." I was done with her, done with everything. Out of desperation, I gave Autumn an ultimatum and suddenly said, "Come to church with me or we're over." I wasn't going to church myself at the time, but it was the only thing I could think of. She reluctantly agreed and we went on a Wednesday night in January of 1999.

The church was called the Christian Life Center in Dayton, Ohio, where they have church services on Wednesdays and Sundays. We had a great evening, and when we went back again, we received a pamphlet about the Alpha course. It said, "If you want an introduction to Christianity, join Alpha, where no question is too simple." I managed to persuade Autumn to do it, as I thought it would be really good for both of us.

So in February 1999, we started the course. At the same time, we both decided to stop drinking, which made the first four or five weeks of the course very difficult. It was a real effort. There were about a hundred people split into groups of eight to ten. We had supper at our table and then listened to the talks given by the pastor, Pete Bryant, who was excellent. Then the weekend retreat came up, and Autumn was very hesitant as she didn't really want to go away for a weekend with people she didn't know that well.

But I persuaded her to see the whole course through, so she agreed to go. However, when the time came to go and we were getting ready to leave, she got mad and said, "Go by yourself. Tell me all about it when you get back." She came up with all these excuses like she had to work and couldn't get child-care for the children. Then, thankfully, at the last minute, a girl at work volunteered to take days off and look after our children, so in the end we both went.

On the retreat the food was great and the teaching was great. They prayed for the Holy Spirit to come and Rick, the guy leading my group, reached out his hand to pray for me. After a few minutes the Holy Spirit hit me, and I started praying in this new language. It was amazing. I surrendered everything to God. I still had so much bitterness in me, but I asked for forgiveness and said, "Lord, I totally surrender to you my bitterness, my anger—everything that's built up over the years." I had to forgive the pastor from the previous church I attended where I had been hurt, as well as a few other people.

I then left the building and went walking out in the woods. I walked up a gravel road praising God in this new language that was so angelic. All I was thinking about was Jesus. I was just praising Him. Words can't describe it. It felt like I was in heaven!

Autumn was still inside and afterward she told me that the table leader came over to pray for her. She cried a lot and became a Christian then and there. At the end of the weekend, we didn't want to leave. We both changed so much on that weekend. The drive home was so beautiful, so peaceful, and there was real unity between Autumn and myself. She was a different lady. Suddenly we could communicate with each other without getting angry.

One night toward the end of the course, Pete, our pastor, sat down with us at dinner and asked if we had thought about marriage, and we said, "No." He told us that if we ever did want to, then he would be proud to have the honor of marrying us. He could have been very judgmental, but he wasn't. He was so gracious and that showed Christ to me. His actions had a real impact on us, and we decided we would marry after all. When Alpha had finished, Autumn and I started talking about all the bitterness between us and started being able to forgive one another. God gave us new hope. We started praying with each other and with the children.

We were married on January 15, 2000, in a small chapel at church by our pastor, Stan Tharp, and it was a very happy occasion. We sent out invitations and probably 70 or 80 percent were people we met through Alpha.

We've all changed so much. Now we go to church as a family all the time and the children love it. Autumn is continually being healed of hurt areas in her life, and I can see it daily. I can see such a change in her. It's a miracle. She used to worry so much, every second her mind was full of worry. She was totally consumed with worry, and now she's 90 percent better.

I've changed as well although I've still got a long way to go. I don't drink anymore, and my vocabulary has cleaned up a lot. I was such an angry and abusive person. I would swear a lot. I think it started with the fact that I was the youngest of three boys and I had to fight to survive with my older brothers. I would even push Autumn sometimes, but none of that has happened since becoming a Christian. I'm now trying to let Jesus be my model in loving my enemies. It's very hard to do when somebody insults you or talks about you, but now I try to give it to God and pray for them instead of wanting to punch them. Autumn and I read the Bible a lot and we try to explain it to our children.

I don't have the words to describe what Jesus means to me. Any words would just be too cheap. I wouldn't be here if it weren't for Him. He's my first love, my destiny, my everything.

"I could see my neighbors doing so well and then I'd look at my home and it was dysfunctional..."

AUTUMN'S STORY

Doug and I got back together in 1998. I was working in financing for a large company, and I would hide my drinking from my coworkers and my employer. I was very angry at the time, very angry at God after my mother died unexpectedly and then my younger brother. I would shout at God, "Why? What kind of God are you?"

Then, in December of 1999, Doug gave me an ultimatum: "You come to church with me or we're over." And so, dragging a ball and chain, I went to church with him. I didn't want to talk to God; I didn't want to talk to Doug. I just wanted to go out and drink. In my mind I considered that Doug and I were through, but to make him happy, I would go to church the one time. So we went the one time and I walked in and felt very welcome there. I had not been in a church for probably 22 years, and I loved the place and the prayer and the teaching that night. So I thought, *That wasn't too bad. I'll go back again.* And that was when we received a pamphlet about this Alpha course.

We joined Alpha not only to learn about a relationship with God, but to meet people. When we started going to church, we both quit drinking totally. When the weekend retreat was mentioned, I thought, *The last thing I want to do is go away for a weekend with people I don't even know.* I didn't want to go to the retreat at all. I kept making all of these excuses. I told Doug I had to work; I told him I couldn't find child-care for my children. Then I told him I wasn't feeling well, and he should go alone and come home and tell me about it. But then, a girl at work volunteered to take days off so that I could make it, and we went to the retreat.

When we got to the weekend and they invited the Holy Spirit to come, Doug and I both cried a lot. I think it was constant crying. I turned into a puddle when I confessed. The table leader came over to pray with me, and I started confessing all the wrong I had done—the drinking, the disobedience to God, not being a very good mother, my alcohol abuse. I got down on my knees and I was crying and praying and asking for forgiveness and thanking God for carrying me through it all. Even though I was attending church, I don't feel that I had actually accepted Christ in my heart till that weekend. I said a prayer, asking for God's forgiveness and asking Him to come into my heart and to guide me down the right path.

Doug is not so violent now. Before we started going to church, I saw many remote controls end up smashed against the wall—many fits of rage.

I had always thought God must have favorites. I could see my neighbors doing so well, and then I'd look at my home and it was dysfunctional—my children were disobedient, my family was dying off, and He wasn't doing anything for me that I could see. I thought, *Well, you are a vengeful God who shows favoritism, and I don't want any part of that.* Now I see I was being disobedient to God. How could I expect my children to be obedient to me if I wasn't doing the right things myself? Now I realize that throughout all the dark moments of my life when I thought He was punishing me, God was there with me. He carried me.

I still can't believe that Jesus would die on the cross so that I could live. Jesus, I now see, is kind, forgiving, loving, and merciful. His is an unending love, and He is always there.

Doug and Autumn Riffle remain active churchgoers. Doug says, "Autumn and I are continuously learning and growing in our faith. It has at times been a rocky journey, but well worth every mile. We thank God each day for His presence in our lives."

"Time and again in our marriage I used to get mad and shout and yell, but I could never really pinpoint why I was angry."

THE STORY OF JERRY AND PAT SWIMM

For 48 years, Jerry Swimm, of Lakeville, Massachusetts, flew into furious rages with his wife, Pat, a regular churchgoer. It became worse when they retired in the 1990s. By early 2001, she had had enough and discussed leaving him. Then God intervened in a way which has astonished them both.

JERRY'S STORY

My mother and father divorced when I was eight and I stayed with my mom. My dad was a heavy drinker, and it was not a happy upbringing really. I was often in trouble and whenever the police came to the door, my mom would think, *Oh, no, what's Jerry been up to now?* In my teens I got quite involved with the Salvation Army and made some friends there, but all that stopped when I left school at the age of 17.

I met Pat on a blind date. A friend asked me to take her out because his girlfriend had come back from summer camp early. We went to a movie together. That was July 1, and we were married on September 27—so it all happened quite quickly. We were married in a Congregational church in Middleboro, Massachusetts, which was Pat's home church. She was 18 and I was 19. After getting married, we went to church together four or five times, and then I stopped because I lost interest. Pat never stopped going and all our children—Jerry Jr., Stephanie, Lindy, Christopher, and Andrea—were brought up in the Congregational church.

I worked hard and wasn't at home much, particularly when I started skin diving around 1965. I did a lot of drinking in those days too; in fact, I was probably very close to being an alcoholic. I would drink in bars, which is what my father used to do. I was a beer drinker for a while, but later went on to the hard stuff, particularly Cinnamon Schnapps.

It was a very stressful time for Pat, who was looking after the children. I would shout at her like nobody's business. I was a bit like Jekyll and Hyde. When I was nasty, I would aggravate her so much that she would get angry with me and start shouting back. I would know it was time to stop, but sometimes I didn't stop—don't ask me why. I can't say I did it to make myself feel better. It was just a spontaneous thing. I now know she was very frightened of me during those years, although I didn't realize it at the time.

When she went to church, I would sit at home and watch the ball game or would be away skin diving. Occasionally, I would go at Easter and Christmas, but for me it was just some place to be. I found it boring and it had nothing for me really. Sometimes Pat would say, "Why don't you come to church?"

I would say, "Well, I've got the gardening to attend to. I've gotta weed the beets." That's a job where I would have to get down on my hands and knees and pick out all the weeds. She knew it took a long time, so she'd drop the subject. When she had gone, I would go out and do a little weeding so that I could say on her return that I had weeded some of the beets because I didn't want to lie. I would never outright lie to her, but I often told her a lot of half-truths. I used to have a knack of saying things in a way that would turn things around completely to my advantage. It was a tool and it worked.

From around 1990—as we both neared retirement—we argued more and more. It would often happen when we were in the car together. One example was when we were driving back from Vermont from a holiday in the early 90s. I got into some heavy traffic and I said to Pat, "You've got the map. Is there an alternate route we could use?"

She said, "No, there isn't."

I shouted, "Whaddaya mean? There's got to be another route!" That sort of thing happened every time we went on a trip. She was the navigator and I was the pilot, but the pilot couldn't cope with the navigator.

Time and again in our marriage I used to get mad and shout and yell, but I could never really pinpoint why I was angry. I must have been or I wouldn't have been shouting, but I didn't know why. Sometimes it may have been the drink, but I stopped drinking around 1985 and my temper didn't improve particularly. In August of 2000 we were growing more and more disagreeable with each other. Pat had said several times that she didn't think she could cope any more and that she was thinking of moving out. My reply was,

"Well, if you want me to move out, I'll move out. I don't care." That was the attitude I took, but I didn't really mean it. I don't think either of us wanted to separate after all those years, but it had become a real possibility. We were talking about it more and more.

In January of 2001 Pat mentioned that she was going to this Alpha course at the church on Sunday nights. She asked me if I minded and I said, "No, go ahead." I wasn't even curious. She went off leaving me in front of the idiot tube, and when she got back, I don't remember her saying much about it. I didn't really know what it was about, and I wasn't interested. Then, one day in March—a nice quiet day after she had finished the course—she came to me and said, "We have to talk."

I said, "OK."

She said, "I want you to go with me to counseling with Pastor Thelma—the pastor of the church."

I said, "OK." I thought our marriage was coming to an end, and my attitude was that you don't throw away forty-seven years without trying.

We went to the meeting with Pastor Thelma, and I loved her right from the minute we started talking. We discussed our problems and some of the things we had done in the past—things Pat had forgiven me for and things I had forgiven her for. By the end, we really had come to some sort of peace over the whole thing. Then Pastor Thelma said to me, "Would you come to the Alpha course?"

If Pat had asked me to go, I don't think I would have done it. But this was Pastor Thelma, so I said, "I'll come to the first one and if I don't want to come back again . . . No promises, no guarantees, no strings, no requirements. If I like it, I'll come back, but if I don't, I won't."

Then Pastor Thelma said, "Let's say a prayer," and she prayed for both of us. So I went along to the first Alpha night. I think there were 12 or 13 people there, and Pat was involved as a helper. We had a meal that was provided by one of the parishioners. I really liked the people there. There was a young fellow and an older couple who really caught my interest, so I even began to look forward to going to the second week.

I enjoyed the second evening of the course as well, but on the Saturday after that, Pat and I had a fight. It was the night before Mother's Day, and we were playing cards with some friends. I was moody and Pat knew I wasn't happy. She asked me what was the matter and I swore at her. I have a knack of doing the wrong thing. After that, there was a kind of silence in the room. After we got home and we'd gone to bed, I said to Pat, "You know, I think we undid everything that the course has done so far. Good night and go to sleep."

I got up the next morning and told Pat I wanted the car while she was at church, so I took her down to the church and drove back home as I had done so many times. When I got home, I began to think about a new desire to change which was awakening in me. I said to myself, "You made yourself a promise which I think you should keep." Then I did something I don't normally do. I got dressed in a suit with a tie and drove to church. There, I sat right at the back. I could see Pat down at the front playing the piano. She didn't see me until about halfway through the service. Then she looked up and saw me, and I could tell. After the service, I went down and gave her a hug. I knew I had done something real special for her, and when I left the church that day, I felt good for her. I felt joy for her.

That Tuesday I went to Alpha. They knew I had gone to church, and I don't think I have had more hugs and kisses in my life. The following Sunday, I got dressed in my suit and went to church again. This time I felt joy not just for Pat, but for myself too. I felt better about being there.

Then came the course weekend. We were supposed to go away, but it didn't work out, so we had it at the church. That was when I started to feel that Christ had found me again. Thelma prayed with another fellow for both of us. Then we each prayed among ourselves, and I quietly prayed for God to come into my life. I didn't tell Pat (I wanted to be sure that something had happened before telling her I had become a Christian), but after we left there, I really felt much, much better. I felt cleansed—better about life and better toward my wife.

After that, things between us improved considerably. When we went to visit our daughter in Virginia in June, she said to us afterward, "That was the best time I have ever had with you two." That was because I wasn't jumpy, I wasn't nasty, and we weren't picking on each other.

Now our relationship just keeps improving. Every day is more beautiful than the last. I pray every day. I get up in the morning, take my medication, brew my coffee, and go and sit down in my chair. There, I read the Bible. I read a bit from the New Testament, then go to a psalm, and then go back to the section in my Bible which gives references for "meaningful prayer." Then I say a silent prayer. I close my eyes and pray for guidance and for help with my family problems. Then I stop and just let my mind go blank. Some day, real soon, I know I am going to hear God speak to me.

I never thought of Jesus as my Savior—until now. Now I know Jesus is love, God is love, and there is nothing so warm as having God's arms around you. Pat and I are now more in love than we have ever been. Why? Because Jesus has come into my heart.

"We really were enemies and I was frightened of him."

PAT'S STORY

Jerry and I really were enemies and I was frightened of him. I was 18 and Jerry 19 when we married. Within ten years, we had five children, and I was a stressed out mother. Jerry remembers those years as relatively happy, but I don't remember them being happy. He never seemed to be there when I needed him. He was working a lot and he went out a lot. At different times we seemed to have a pretty good life, but he was often verbally abusive to me.

When I reached the age of 38 or 40, I was able to go to work, and when I did that I felt as if I were more of a person in my own right. I never knew what would upset him. It got better for a while after he stopped drinking. He was never physically abusive, but I always had this fear of him, because I didn't want to aggravate him into striking me. My mother was a big help. She would say, "Don't aggravate him. Let him go on." She was his greatest ally.

The real bickering came in the last ten years. Then Jerry retired in 1997 and I retired in March 2000. But it got to the point where we couldn't take a trip. It was a rare thing to take a trip without one blow up where he would scream and holler so much that people outside the car could hear. I would read the map and he would say, "Well which way do we turn? I've gotta go! I've gotta go!"

We would go through periods of fairly happy times and then it would deteriorate. I felt that Jerry must be very, very angry at something or someone. Every time we went through these things I thought, *I can't take any more of this. I can't stand it.*

In January of 2001 I signed up for the Alpha course at church. I thought it would help deepen my spirituality and give me a focus. I didn't expect Jerry to take it. He had been growing more hardened in his attitude toward the church, and he was very stubborn.

The course was a new experience for me. I really enjoyed it, even though I had been a Christian all of my life. I knew I needed something. During the Holy Spirit session, I prayed with all my heart that Jerry would come to Christ. I had no hope of that happening—no rational or logical hope that that would happen. But I thought, *This is the last resort for us, and he needs Christ in his life.*

Then, the following Sunday, Pastor Thelma preached a sermon on forgiveness—forgiving your enemies. I thought Jerry had been literally my enemy all these years. We really were enemies. There had been very little love between us, even though we did love each other and he had his good moments. I went up to Pastor Thelma and said, "Your sermon meant a great deal to me today and I am going to forgive my husband. I realize I need to do that."

She said, "I provide counseling, you know."

And I said, "Well, I want to make an appointment."

When I got home, Jerry seemed less argumentative so I thought, *Well, I'll take whatever I can get.* I asked him if he would come for counseling and he said yes. I was so excited when he said he would do one session—and then when he continued to go.

But then came a big fight the night before Mother's Day. It was quick, like all of them. He is very quick tempered when he blows up. We were playing cards with two or three other people, and when he turned on me, there was silence in the room. Everybody was startled when he swore and went into a silence. Then he came to church the following day, and that was when everything really began to change. It has been amazing. He never told me he had invited Christ into his life until quite a time afterward, but I knew.

Now we are more in love than we have ever been. I now look at him and think, *Now, this is the man I married.*

Jerry and Pat Swimm are members of The Central United Methodist Church in Middleboro. Jerry is a regular member of a men's prayer group and says, "I have not missed a Sunday in church since Mother's Day, 2001. What wonderful things have filled my life!"

"It was like my life was weighed down with many, many weights—steel weights—on my shoulders."

5

THE STORY OF FRANK COSTA

New York firefighter Frank Costa, 33, was "feeling very depressed and didn't know what to do" before going to an Alpha course in 1998, after which he committed his life to Jesus Christ. Then, three years later, came September 11. Here he tells the story.

I was brought up in New York City in a Catholic family. When I was a child, my mother took me—and my brother—to church every Sunday. My father didn't go. The churchgoing tapered off when I was about 12 years old, after I got out of eighth grade. After that, I didn't go any more.

After college, I got my own apartment and got a job. I was out in the world, dating different women. If I wanted to bring a girlfriend back to my apartment for the night, it wasn't a problem for me. Exploring my sexuality was just a natural instinct. For the first few years, I worked as the director of a gym and fitness facility—the pool and the recreation area—at the Marriott Hotel. But I always wanted to be a New York City firefighter and had my name down for a long time awaiting their call-up. Becoming a firefighter isn't easy. You have to be a certain age, in good health, and able to do well on a test. It's a long, drawn-out process.

Around February of 1998, I was feeling very depressed. For a few years I had been living with a girl, and it wasn't working out. I knew I was the problem and didn't know what to do. It was then that I bumped into an old friend, Anthony Acierno, walking his dog in Queens where I live. He had been my roommate some years before, when we were 23 or 24 years old, but I hadn't seen much of him since. In those days he had been interested in a search for God and had been investigating Christianity.

He asked how I was, and I told him something was wrong in my life. I said I felt very, very sad and I didn't really know why. That was when he said some words which were to have huge significance in my life. He said, "There is a course at my church called Alpha, and it's starting in a couple of weeks. Why don't you take it? I've been on it and it helped me a tremendous amount."

I said, "Are you sure this course is OK?" Being a New

THE STORY OF FRANK COSTA

Yorker, I'm very suspicious about everything. I was concerned that it may be some kind of cult.

He said, "No, this course is the truth. You should check it out."

So, because he was such a good friend of mine, I went along.

The course was held at a church in another part of Queens on Wednesday nights at seven o'clock. For the first night, Anthony went with me. There were maybe 45 to 50 people, and I was still suspicious.

But I enjoyed the talk and at the end—before we got into our groups to discuss it—the pastor asked if anybody wanted to pray silently as they sat. He said, "If you would like to make peace with God at this time, you might want to repeat this prayer silently to God." I suddenly felt I wanted to do as he said.

He said a prayer like: "Dear Lord, I admit I've lived my life in a way that You would not have approved of and I am sorry. I turn away from everything that I have done that You are not happy with. I acknowledge and accept that Jesus died for my sins on the cross, and that He paid the price for my sins. I receive that in my life now, and I ask You to come into my life and be a part of my life."

As he spoke it, I said the prayer quietly just as he suggested and found myself very moved. It was like my life was weighed down with many, many weights—steel weights—on my shoulders. But after saying the prayer, it was as if several of those weights had been taken right off me. I was put in a group, and everybody seemed very friendly. After that night, I said the same prayer again and again. Every time I said the prayer it was like taking a shower. As I asked God for forgiveness, it felt as if I was getting cleaner and cleaner.

I went along the second and third weeks and enjoyed the course more and more, but I still wasn't going to church. I wasn't quite ready for that. Then, the week after that, after just three weeks of the course, I was called into the Fire Academy. Prospective firefighters have to attend a 13-week intensive training course at the Academy, and it consumes every moment of your time for three months, so I had to stop Alpha. I was falling asleep at home with my study books in my lap. They drain you completely to become a New York City fireman. But by the end, I was qualified and started work.

In February of 1999, after a painful time in which I broke up with my girlfriend, I asked my friend Anthony whether the Alpha course was happening again, and he said it was. So this time I took the course in its entirety. I had a lot of questions, and the leader didn't avoid answering my questions, but he allowed others to join in the debate. At some point in the middle of the course, I started going to church, and my Christian faith really began to get stronger after that.

There was a period of time where I was saying, "I'm exploring Christianity," and then I remember feeling that I couldn't possibly ever go back. I realized I wasn't exploring Christianity any more. I was a Christian.

I am not an impulsive person. I do everything methodically. So for me it was a very gradual process. Some people dive into Christianity and it works for them, but with me it happened very, very steadily. Gradually I became more and more committed. My prayer life became much more sincere. I found myself really conversing with God. God had not changed, but my perception of Him had completely changed.

By this time, I had a new girlfriend, Angie, but she wasn't a Christian, and I wasn't sure if it would be right to continue the relationship. I invited her to come to the next Alpha Course and she just loved it and became a Christian as well. Now we are planning to get married later in the year.

Before doing the course, I thought it was an honorable thing for Jesus to die on the cross, but it wasn't entirely necessary. Afterward, I finally understood that Jesus chose to do what He did . . . for me. And I desperately needed Him to do that. All of a sudden I realized that Jesus—His role in my life—was infinitely important.

On September 9, 2001, I was at a fire in Brooklyn. I was getting into the truck to get more equipment when I accidentally sprained my left ankle as I got out. The pain was so bad I thought I was going to pass out. It was the first time I had really hurt myself at a fire. Two days later, I had an early morning appointment with the Fire Department doctor in Brooklyn, right across the water from the World Trade Center. The doctor checked out my ankle and said, "Well, it's obvious you're not going to be able to work. Come back next week and we'll see if the swelling has gone down."

In the waiting room there were television sets and news-papers, and there was a woman there yelling and making a big commotion. I looked at the TV and saw a live picture from a helicopter of one of the World Trade Center towers on fire, with a tremendous amount of black smoke coming out of it. Then, right before our eyes—live on TV from this helicopter camera—we saw a huge plane go right into the other tower. There were others in the waiting room, and no one said anything. We didn't understand what we were watching. We were totally in shock. Then somebody said, "Was that an instant replay?" Finally the grim reality set in that this was a terrorist attack.

I got into the car (which was difficult to drive because I have manual transmission, but I could just do it) and went home, where I heard there was a "total recall," which means that all firefighters need to go back to their fire-house. I called my firehouse and asked my lieutenant, "Do you need me to come back?" But he told me to stay home, because he knew I was injured and there was just too much going on. So I watched everything on television that day. My ladder company —Ladder Company 142—did not go down to the World Trade Center until later that evening, because they were in Queens [across the Hudson River from Manhattan]. Many, many companies went, but ours was told to remain on stand-by.

Being a fireman I know that when there's a fire, many people are running out of a building, but we are doing the exact opposite. We are running in as fast as they're running out. I've been to fires in skyscrapers (of course, nothing like the World Trade Center), and we were able to put them out. So when I saw those buildings come down, I just started crying. I knew I was witnessing the deaths of many, many people, including many fire-fighters, many police officers, and ambulance workers.

We lost one guy from my firehouse, Ray York, who had an injured shoulder and was based in Manhattan speaking to tourists and children about being a fireman. On September 11 he saw what happened and hitched a ride in a van down to the World Trade Center to see if he could help. He died as he was helping people out there.

My brother is a firefighter in Manhattan, and he lost six firefighters from his fire company. Everyone from his company who went down to the World Trade Center that day died. And so my brother's struggling right now. They have just found a couple of their bodies, and that has reopened all the wounds.

I don't know what my reaction would have been had this happened during a time when I was not a Christian. At first I felt that I was a bad example to the men that I work with because I became very, very depressed. I didn't want to do anything but pray.

But now I have realized that Jesus wept. Jesus grieved. So if Jesus had to experience grief, then I knew it was normal for me to do the same, and He would give me the strength to endure it.

Frank Costa and his fiancée, Angie, continue to attend St. John Evangelical Lutheran Church in Glendale, Queens, New York.

"There were days when I felt things
were never going to get better."

6

THE STORY OF SANDY AND TONY VENTURA

One day in June, 1991, Sandy and Tony Ventura accepted the invitation of some family friends to go on a boat trip with their young sons, Matthew and Nicholas. It was to be a day of tragedy. Here Sandy Ventura describes what happened and how God reached out to her in her despair.

SANDY'S STORY

As a child, I went to the local Catholic church with my mom and dad. I kept going even as a young adult but then kind of fell away from it. At the age of 23 I found myself pregnant. The church tried to persuade us to wait until after the baby was born to get married, but I thought it best to be married before the baby was born, so we were married by a Justice of the Peace.

My son, Matthew, was born in June of 1985, and when he was only six months old, I left my husband. He had a drug habit and was physically abusive toward me. He threatened to hurt my son also, so I left and moved back with my parents. In 1986, when Matthew had just turned a year old, I met a man named Tony. He had actually been my high school crush, but after we graduated, we went our separate ways. We dated for a while and married in 1988. Tony was like my "knight in shining armor." He not only loved me, but he also accepted Matthew as if he were his own son.

In 1989, our son Nicholas was born. The experience of his birth was so different because I was in a loving relationship. Tony was totally involved in every part of my pregnancy and the birth. My whole world seemed to change after Nicholas was born. I finally felt my life was coming together. Nicholas always seemed to be too-good-to be true from the moment he was born. I know every parent must feel this way about their children, but Nicholas had an extra special little personality for his young age. In the midst of all this happiness and contentment, I never had any idea what trials still lay ahead for us.

One day in June 1991, when Matthew was six and Nicholas 22 months, we were invited as a family to go on a friend's boat to Chesapeake City, Maryland. It was a last-minute invite and, Tony called me at work to say, "Do you want to go on this boat ride?"

I was kind of reluctant because I felt Nicholas was too young and wouldn't sit still. But it got to the point where I felt I was being a bit of a party pooper, so I said, "OK, let's go." It was a 22-foot cabin cruiser. There were nine of us on board that day. Our friends had two children of their own and a niece that was visiting with them. Our destination was a restaurant owned by my sister and her husband called Dock Side Yacht Club.

We arrived there, had lunch, and then set off for the journey home as it was getting dark. About eight that night, I was downstairs in the bottom cabin with Nicholas and Matthew and our friends' two boys—ages five and eight—when suddenly we heard all this screaming and yelling from above. I went to the cabin door to see what the commotion was when Tony appeared with his arms stretched out and yelled, "Sandy, give me the baby."

I handed him Nicholas and within seconds there was this huge crash, and I was totally submerged underwater with things hitting me on the head and flipping around. We had been hit by a barge which was being operated with no lights. We had no chance of getting out of the way. I fought to get to the surface and finally found a way up out of the water. The boat had flipped over, and I was trapped under the boat in an air pocket with about 18 inches of room to breathe. There was just about enough space for my head to be out of the water. Somehow, our friends' two sons ended up trapped in the same air pocket with me, but all I could hear of Matthew was that he was just screaming and screaming for me. It was very dark, and he was trapped in a separate air pocket. All three children were wearing life jackets.

Matthew continued screaming for me, but I couldn't get to him so I just tried to calm him down with my voice. He kept saying, "Something's crushing me, Mommy." It was complete torture to hear him screaming for help and not be able to do anything to help him. We discovered later he was trapped in one of the compartments where boating equipment was kept.

I was scared to death and convinced we were all just waiting to die, because it would only be a matter of time before we would run out of air and the boat would sink. I started banging real hard on the bottom of the boat because I could hear my husband's voice outside. He and the other passengers had been thrown overboard when the collision occurred. He reassured me that help was on its way.

Once the coastguards arrived, they put air bags under the boat to keep it afloat so that they could drag us into shallow water. There they worked for almost four hours carefully trying to figure out the best and safest way to get us out. They were concerned that if they cut a hole in the top of the boat it would release the air and we would sink.

Through all this time, I was talking to my husband, who

was crying. He didn't mention Nicholas once, and I didn't ask him because I could just tell by the sound of his voice that Nicholas was gone. I tried everything in my power not to lose my composure, because that was the only thing that was keeping the other children from panicking.

The divers came under to try to get us out and decided to get Matthew into the air pocket with us. First, they had to convince him to take off his life jacket, because he said, "My mom told me never to take my life jacket off." I told him it was OK this one time, but he had a big fear of going underwater. It took a long while to persuade him to hold his nose and go underwater. Miraculously, they got him under the water and into our air pocket, and then they proceeded to cut the hole in the boat above our heads. That done, they lifted us out one at a time.

As soon as I got out, I said, "Where's my baby?" Everyone was so concerned about warming us up because we had been in the water for so long (they were worried about hypothermia) that they didn't answer. I was too weak and in shock to fight. There were helicopters flying around, and I saw Tony sitting in a lifeboat. He was just crying out loud saying, "I tried to hold onto him. I tried, but I just couldn't hold him." I knew then Nicholas was gone.

Later I learned that the collision had thrown Tony and Nicholas into the water, where Tony held on to him underwater trying to get to the surface. But the turbulence was too strong, and they were pulled underneath the barge. Every time Tony tried to reach the surface he kept hitting his head on the bottom of the barge. And all the time he was getting drawn closer and closer to the back of the barge where he could hear the propellers. He said that was when the water ripped Nicholas out of his hands. Tony rose to the surface and was pulled out of the water by someone who had been passing by.

Nicholas had been wearing a life jacket earlier in the journey, but I had just taken it off to change his diaper. They didn't recover his body for two days. Our friend, Tommy, who owned the boat and whose sons I was trapped under the boat with, also died. One of his sons, Matthew, had told me as we were together under the boat: "As soon as I get out of here, I'm going to give my daddy the biggest kiss and hug."

At the time I didn't know anything had happened to Tommy. After being pulled out of the boat, I saw his wife sitting on the rescue boat, crying, and I realized he was not around. I said, "Where's Tommy?" She just shook her head. I just remember those two boys screaming when they heard their daddy was gone. We were in shock for a long time after the accident.

After the funeral, I reached out to different support groups for parents who have lost a child. It helped me to be able to talk to other parents who had lost children. It was a day-to-day process. But there were also days when I felt like things were never going to get better. Tony was devastated and couldn't go back to work for a long time. He felt it was his fault because he was the last one to have Nicholas in his arms, and he couldn't save him. After some time I started going back to church. I thought maybe this would make me feel better. I also became involved in a support group based on religion and Christianity, but I still did not seem to find what I was looking for. I felt like I was not moving forward.

In 1993, we had a daughter, Gabrielle, and then our second daughter, Jessica, was born in 1995. I continued going to my local Catholic church off and on until March of 2000, but it was more a thing I had to do, instead of a thing I wanted to do. I finally stopped going because I didn't feel like I was getting anything from it. A month later, I decided to check out a new church which had just been built locally—Covenant Fellowship. It was eleven o'clock on a Sunday morning, and I went with my two daughters (my son Matthew was not with me and my husband wasn't going to church that much). I put my girls in childcare, then I sat in the back row.

From the moment the pastor started speaking, I felt like he was speaking directly to me. It brought tears to my eyes. I returned the following Sunday, and they announced that "if you have questions about Jesus or about what happens when you die . . ." (that really caught my attention because I had struggled with that question for so long after the loss of my son) ". . . then we recommend you go to the Alpha course."

It was a course starting on Wednesday nights at the church. So I very much wanted to check it out. I went to the first night and, the whole experience was just awesome. On the second week, I was given the opportunity to pray a prayer asking Jesus into my heart. I prayed along with the leader and asked Jesus to forgive me of all my sins.

From that point, Alpha became the highlight of my week. Everything I learned about Jesus suddenly became so much more personal. The course made Jesus so much more of a real person to me than He was before. About halfway into the course, we went on a retreat. There some people prayed for me to be filled with the Holy Spirit and, as they did so, I felt like crying. I had this awesome feeling of release coming from me. It was as if all the pain and sorrow I had been carrying with me since my son died was taken from me and replaced with this overwhelming sense of peace. Where the Bible had never made sense to me before, I actually now started to understand it. Though I prayed before, it never felt like I was getting anywhere. Now when I pray, I feel like I am actually speaking to God, and that makes me feel closer to Him.

It has meant a total change in my life. Before, I knew I was doing things that were wrong, but I had no strength to stop it—no strength to change. Then, I knew Nicholas was in heaven, and I felt close to him, but there was still something lacking. Now that I am a Christian, I can be so much more at peace knowing that by God's grace and mercy, I can be together with my son again some day in heaven.

I am not saying that I don't still have times when I miss my son. I will always miss him, but God has given me hope and strength which helps make those times a little easier to get through now. God has replaced a lot of the pain with peace, knowing that I can trust in Him and put it all in His hands. I know nothing can ever replace my son, but the peace and love that I have found in the Lord has filled the part of my heart that was taken from me when my son died.

With the strength I have from God, I think I can face anything after what I have been through.

TONY'S STORY

I was constantly being haunted by the same dream of watching my son as he floated out of my arms. My anger at God slowly led me back into my old ways. I was so angry at Him for saving me but not my son. I started using drugs to numb myself to the point where I was a total wreck. My life just started going downhill. After Sandy did the Alpha course, I saw the change in her but I was still mad at God. I felt like now He was trying to take my wife from me too. I even told her at one point to choose me or God.

Eventually, I went to church and attended Alpha. Then things started to happen to me. The look of happiness everyone had, and the love I felt from total strangers was overwhelming. I attended the course retreat and on the Friday night after hearing the talk I went back to my room. At 3:37 in the morning, I awoke out of a dead sleep and just felt the need to start confessing my sins. And me, a lonely sinner, a man who thought even God could not save, asked

Jesus into my heart. I instantly felt like a changed man. The next day on the retreat I was prayed for and felt the Holy Spirit come into my body and fill me. All I could do was cry. At that instant, I realized that God was all I ever needed in the first place.

My life now, as a Christian, is like being given a second chance. I know I still have a long road to travel, but now I know I will never be traveling that road alone. I thank God for saving me, and now I know in my heart that someday I will see my son again in the glorious presence of the Lord.

Sandy and Tony Ventura are now members of Covenant Fellowship Church in Glen Mills, Pennsylvania. Sandy has been serving on the Alpha Task Force and also in children's ministry.

"I felt like nobody understood what I was going through. My daughter didn't understand why I was crying all the time."

THE STORY OF NIKKI PALMA

In June, 1999, Nikki Palma took a call from her best friend, Robin, who had just given birth to twins and said everything was going well. Nikki arranged to visit the next day. But she never spoke to her friend again. Robin collapsed with a brain aneurysm soon afterward. Nikki, grief-stricken, began to wonder if God was there.

I was brought up Catholic. My parents wanted me and my two older brothers to have a religious background, but I didn't like the rules. I thought the church cared more about how people were dressed and whether they were coming in late than about good things. I got a bad taste in my mouth, so I veered away when I got out of high school and stopped going.

When I was 20, I was engaged to my boyfriend when he broke his neck in a football accident. He was a police officer on the police officers' football team. He ran into somebody head on with his helmet and broke his neck. It was very frightening. I slept on two chairs beside him in the hospital for nine days, and I was so grateful to God when he got better that I started trying going to church again. But it didn't last long. We got married and tried to make it work, but it didn't. We only made it for three years, so I got divorced when I was 24 going on 25. I was on my own for a while, but it was a very traumatic time. My parents had been married for 32 years, and they were horrified. Nobody in my family had been divorced.

I became a 911 operator for the fire department and met my current husband at "the River" (the Colorado River where you go boating and water skiing). He is a fireman. His name is Dan, and we got married in 1995 when I was 27. I really wanted to be married in a church, but Dan didn't because he didn't have that background. In the end we were married by a pastor at a Disneyland hotel in Anaheim.

When our daughter, Cassidi, was born, I wanted her to be baptized, so we arranged for that to be in the church I grew up in. It wasn't a very nice baptism though, as the priest was foreign and I couldn't understand him. He wasn't very helpful, and I was kind of put off again. When it was time for Cassidi to start pre-school, I checked around and liked the pre-school at Grace Lutheran Church, Huntington Beach, and she started there in February of 1999.

On a Sunday soon afterward there was a little program she was going to be singing in at church, and I went with my video camera and sat in the front row. I watched her singing and it was wonderful. Then the teachers took the kids out, and the rest of the congregation listened to the sermon. I thought, *Well, what am I supposed to do? Am I supposed to stay here or am I supposed to leave?* Nobody else was getting up, and I was in the front row with my video camera. I decided to stay and listened to the sermon, and it was overwhelming. Pastor John Bradowsky was a wonderful speaker, and by the end, I couldn't wait till the next Sunday to go back.

So I did and while I was there I found a flyer in the pew pocket about a program called Alpha, which was described as "an opportunity to explore." There was also a big sign outside the church saying, "Alpha's here." I thought, *What is Alpha? Am I the only one who doesn't know?* Then I got some information in the mail about it, explaining that it was free and an opportunity to learn in a non-threatening atmosphere, which I liked. So I thought, *I want to go to this and learn more.* But my husband didn't want to go, and I didn't know anybody at church and didn't want to go by myself. Then I ran into some friends of my husband's, Dennis and Sandy Cross, who said they were thinking of going to the course. I said, "Really? I'll go if you guys go." So we all sat together.

There were about 50 people there and I enjoyed the video and the friendship, so I kept going back. I didn't go on the Holy Spirit weekend because my brother got married, but I finished the course. Nothing life-changing happened to me, but I enjoyed it.

The day before our celebration dinner my best friend,

Robin Law, delivered twins. It was a real surprise because they were two months early, but as soon as they were born, she called me. I was one of the first people she called. She told me they were a boy and a girl—Landon and Lexis—and I asked her how they were. She said, "They're fine. They took them right away, but they told me they are fine."

I asked, "And you?" She said she was doing fine too and everything was great.

I said, "I'll call you tomorrow and plan on coming to visit you."

I thought that I would have to leave it a day because of the course celebration dinner, and Robin lived about 35 miles from me. The next day I kept calling the hospital, but there was no answer from Robin's room when I gave the number. So in the evening, when I was ironing my dress for the celebration dinner, I finally called and asked for her by name and the receptionist was really kind of odd. She asked if I was a family member, and I said, "No, I am a really good friend. What's up?"

She said, "Let me just put you through to the waiting room phone."

I said, "Oh, is she visiting with her family?"

She said, "Just let me do that."

It was busy and she came back and said, "You know, honey, I can't get ahold of anyone."

And I said, "What's wrong? What area are you ringing me?"

She said, "ICU." [Intensive Care Unit]

So I thought immediately something had happened to

the twins because they were two months early. The operator said, "Let me put you through again." So she rang it, and Robin's sister-in-law answered the phone.

I said, "This is Nikki here. What's wrong?"

She said, "Oh, my goodness, we have been trying to get ahold of you. Heidi [Robin's sister] didn't have your phone number. Let me have her talk to you."

There was a pause and then she said, "She's not here. I can't find her."

By this time I was getting really nervous. I said, "What's wrong? Is something wrong with the babies?"

"No, something is wrong with Robin."

I said, "What is wrong with Robin?"

"She has had a brain aneurysm."

I screamed, "Oh my God. Is she OK?"

"No."

I said, "I need to talk to Heidi."

She said, "I can't find her. Give me your phone number and I'll have her call you back."

Heidi called me back about five minutes later. She was crying.

I said, "What is going on? What is wrong?"

She said, "Robin has had a brain aneurysm, and they have just done a CAT scan [a brain scan] and she has no brain activity. Basically she is dead."

I said, "Oh my God! How did this happen? What is going on? She has just had twins." I was hysterical, but I said I would be there at once.

I called my mom at work, and she just said, "Stay there.

Don't drive. Your dad will come and get you."

She called my dad at work, and he came and got me. They live quite close to the hospital—Arcadia Methodist Hospital—and we went back to their house, and Cassidi stayed with dad while mom and I went to the hospital. We went in, and I spoke with Robin's husband and her mom and sister. I am close to them, and they were glad to see me. They said, "You have to go and see her, but it's not good." So I went in the room, and her dad was in there and he was glad to see me too. Robin looked like she was sleeping, but she was gone. She had a tube to keep her breathing. The doctors said, "We are going to wait 24 hours before we do another CAT scan and see if there's any brain activity, and if there isn't, we will have to try and take her off the life support."

I was hysterical, as was Robin's sister, who is a close friend too. She would grab on to me and just cry, and, of course, I would cry, but I was trying to comfort her also. It transpired that Robin had delivered the twins at around 8:15 at night and she had called me at 8:31 exactly. Then her husband, parents, and in-laws came to the hospital and took pictures before leaving her for the night. That night she had a terrible headache and couldn't sleep. She kept calling the nurse, who asked, "Do you want something to help you sleep?" She said no until three a.m. when she couldn't take it any more, and she said yes. So they gave her something to sleep.

She woke up the next morning and was eating breakfast at about eight o'clock, when she suddenly went into a respiratory arrest and stopped breathing. The doctors came in and put the tube in her mouth to help her breathe. Some time afterward they did the CAT scan and found that there was no brain activity. That's how they realized that she had had an aneurysm. It was totally unexpected.

I stayed until about three the next morning, then went home for a little sleep before coming back again. At that stage, the doctor said there was no brain activity. The only way she was staying alive was because of the life support. So the family made a decision to take her off.

I was there on that Friday, June 25, 1999, when they turned off the life support. She just looked like she was sleeping. Her hair was pulled back and she looked normal to me, only she didn't open her eyes when we talked to her. All day there had been a whole lot of friends coming and going. At the end it was just another friend, Julie, me, and Robin's sisters, parents, and her in-laws. Steve, her husband, couldn't take it and he left to be with their two older children, who were ages six and eight. They didn't know what was going on. It was six p.m. when we were ready to leave, but I couldn't get up. I felt I couldn't leave without her. It was terrible.

They had the funeral at the Catholic church that I grew up in. Robin didn't grow up Catholic, but her husband was Catholic, so they baptized her in the hospital and gave her her last rites. I spoke at her funeral. I let people know who she was to me and what kind of person she was. She was friends with so many people. She was three years older than me but she always protected me. So I spoke about her being my protector and how we talked on the telephone five times a day up to the day she died.

After the funeral I got really depressed, more depressed than I could comprehend, and I didn't know what to do or where to turn. I called my pastor, John, as I was still going to church every Sunday. I wasn't mad at God, but I needed to understand. I was having a hard time getting up in the morning and felt as if I just wanted to go right back to bed and stay there. My daughter didn't understand why I was crying all the time. I felt like nobody understood what I was going through. My husband wanted to go and see a movie or go out to dinner, but I couldn't do anything. I just felt so isolated and alone.

My sister-in-law, Roxane, who is Dan's sister, is a Christian and very much into religion. She told me to start reading Psalms and gave me a couple of other different Scriptures to read to try to find an answer that I was looking for. Then Gayla, my group leader from the Alpha course, asked me if I would be a helper on the next course. I didn't think I could do it, but I said, "You know what? I'm going to try."

So I went to the leaders' meeting and was surrounded by a bunch of really nice people, and I felt really comfortable. I was surprised how I felt, and I thanked God when I got home. I knew I had Him at my side and I wasn't alone anymore. I didn't care if people didn't understand why I was so sad. He knew, and that's all that mattered.

I went through the course again, and I kept hearing things which helped me directly with my depression over

Robin's death. I just felt overwhelmed with gratitude. I didn't know that God could forgive me for everything that I have done in my life. Now I know that He is loving and that He has been with me all through my grief. My new Christian faith means I am happier than I have been in years—especially with my husband. We couldn't see eye to eye on a lot of things, but now I think he sees the change in me. Now I put time aside to read the Bible, which is something I never used to do. I never used to understand it, but now I do.

People tell me, "You look so happy. You are glowing." I can feel it, and I know it is from God.

Nikki Palma continues to be an active member of her local church. She remains close to Robin's family.

"For many years I felt as if I had a black hole inside me and no matter how much booze I poured down my body, it didn't fill it."

7

THE STORY OF LISA MAUSOLF

Mother of five, Lisa Mausolf of Travers City, Michigan, served five months in jail for driving while intoxicated. With her marriage in trouble and a severe drinking problem, she was invited to a local church.

Although my parents never went to church, our next door neighbor went to an Episcopal church, and I started going with her from the age of nine. By the time I was 14, none of my friends were going to church so I quit.

I met my husband, Jeffrey, at a convenience store while we were in high school. I was just hanging out, talking with friends, when he and his brother came to buy something from the store. We got married when I was 21 and had five children, after which my husband starting going into bars and coming home late every night.

I escaped into my own little world and after a while I started drinking at home by myself. I would just have a beer when the kids went to bed. I began drinking more and more. I figured if he was going to do it, I was going to do it.

In 1993, I was caught DWI [driving while intoxicated], but I kept on driving. I graduated from beer to hard liquor like whisky and vodka. Our fifth child was born in 1994. I was caught DWI a second time and then, in 1996, a third time. After that third time—when I was three times over the legal limit—I was given a year in the county jail.

By the time I went to jail in 1997, I had given up drink, which was not an easy thing to do. In the end, I only served five months of my sentence, but it still felt like a long time. Twelve women shared one large room with no windows and one bathroom. The only way we could exercise was to walk round and round the table in the middle of the room. We were given food three times a day and had our lights turned out at a set time in the evening. We had a television, but we were only allowed out for one 15-minute visit a week.

The only good thing for me was that because of my five children I was allowed out to be with my family on weekends. My children were really excited when they came for their weekly visit on Wednesday nights, but they cried and cried when the time came for them to go. Just before I was due to leave jail, my husband served me with divorce papers. By that stage I had been sober for nearly a year, so I ended up getting custody of the kids and I moved out on my own with the five children.

I came out of jail in March 1998 and soon afterwards my husband wanted me to go back to him. He said the only reason he had filed for divorce was to teach me a lesson.

By this time I was working as a waitress as many hours as I could to pay for the rent and the groceries. The state helped me with day care, which with five kids was a lot of hours a week. I wasn't drinking at all, and my husband told me that he too would quit drinking if I moved back. I wouldn't allow drink near me in the house any more, because I didn't want to go back to that person. I didn't like that person I became.

I moved back and after four or five months, my husband was drinking in front of me again. One night he offered me a drink and said, "Go ahead, have one. It's not going to hurt you." I hesitated, but he added, "I don't care if you get drunk as long as you just stay home and do it." So I started drinking again.

From then on I started to get physically mean because of my drinking. I would attack my husband physically. I didn't do it with the kids, but I would be verbally mean with them. There came a time when the kids wouldn't talk to me. One day I woke up and remembered my dad had told me to pray to God when I was in trouble and He would help me. So that morning I looked up, hung over as can be, and I just said, "God, please help me. Show me what I've got to do."

Within a week I had put myself into a rehab center to quit drinking. My mother-in-law looked after the children and I was there for two weeks. While I was there I met a lady who worked there named Sally Krepps. She was a Christian and after I got out of rehab she said to me, "Why not come and try my church?"

It was a church called Lake Ann Methodist Church and when I went there I liked it at once. The people were so friendly and warm and the pastor was so kind. Then Sally said, "You've got to try Alpha." She said it was a course to help me get to know Christianity better and it was on Thursday nights.

I said, "All right." This was January 1999.

We watched the videos and at the end of the first night there is a prayer where you can give your life to Christ. So I said the prayer. You say sorry for what you have done—and then it gives you a few minutes to tell God what you want to be forgiven for. And then you say something like, "I give my life to Christ." From then on Christ was in my life—totally.

When we went on the course retreat, it was totally awesome. I just cried. For the first time in my life I felt safe. For many years I had felt as if I had a black hole inside me and no matter how much booze I poured down my body, it didn't fill it. And finally, after I don't know how many years, this hole inside me was filled. And it wasn't filled with alcohol, it was filled with Christ.

I went home from the weekend and my husband said almost immediately, "You are different." My kids noticed it too.

Before becoming a Christian I was miserable and I didn't care what happened to me. But now I love life. I love my church and if it weren't for my church I'd probably be right back out there drinking. But I don't even have the desire to do that any more. And my kids are so amazed at me. Now they come to church with me because they've seen what God's done for their mom.

When you're an alcoholic you're selfish. You don't care about nothing and I didn't give my children much thought. I loved them all right, but now they're precious to me. They are everything to me. My husband has seen the difference in me and says he likes the difference. I may still get mad occasionally but I don't blow my stack any more. I am more tranquil.

I used to think Jesus was a fake. Now He has given me my dignity back. I have a love for myself that I had lost years and years ago—and He has given me the love and respect of my children back. He has saved my marriage too because we were on our way to divorce. I would have left by now—I know that.

When I was drinking I gave up on life. I totally gave up on me. I was in a bubble. That was my reality—nobody could hurt me. And now I never ever want to go back there. And thanks to Jesus Christ I won't.

Lisa Mausolf has since been through difficult times. In the same year her mother, father, and eldest brother died, and her youngest son was hit by a car. She says, "If it weren't for my faith in Jesus Christ, I would have drunk myself to death so I couldn't feel all the pain. But thanks to the Lord, I am still here and still sober."

"He tried giving up drinking but he just couldn't. He had been an alcoholic for more than 30 years."

THE STORY OF KAREN AND BRIAN WHALEY

Terribly scarred in a car accident as a teenager, Karen Whaley, of Marietta, Georgia, was married to an alcoholic husband who "would scream and yell and punch holes in the wall." She was frightened for herself and their two daughters. But in 2001 came a miraculous transformation in their family. This is what happened.

KAREN'S STORY

I was an only child and very spoiled. I got in with the wrong people at school—doing drugs and drinking.

One night when I was 15, I had been out with a group of friends when I was involved in a car accident. There were three of us in the car, a Ford Pinto, and we were coming home from a party all drunk. The guy who was driving, who was my boyfriend at the time, lost control of the car and hit a telegraph pole. I was in the front seat and didn't have my seat belt on. I fell out of the car and got stuck underneath with the exhaust in my mouth and against my arm. It was terribly hot and burned my nose off, as well as my top lip, my bottom lip, and the side of my face. For a long while nobody knew I was there because my boyfriend was drunk and was trying to not get arrested. He didn't get hurt and neither did the girl in the back seat—but he never told anybody that I had been in the car. I was unable to shout because my mouth was against the exhaust. It was only when they came to tow the car away that someone saw me and said, "Look, there's a person under this!" I don't know how long I had been there.

That was in 1980, and it was a defining moment in my life. From then on, I no longer looked—I won't say "normal" because normal is a word I don't like—from then on I looked different from other people. During the next five years, I had 78 operations. They had to create a new nose from the skin on my arm and a new top lip from skin on my hip. My bottom lip came from my neck. I can't say I was mad at God, because He didn't even exist for me. But it was horrible. At school, the other kids made my life so miserable that I didn't go to school at all in my senior year, but stayed at home with a tutor. I remained friends with the people I knew from before my accident, but I couldn't make new friends because of how I looked. I had never been a very outgoing person, but I certainly became a more "behind the scenes" person.

After my accident, I was always aware of how I looked. I knew it was on everybody's mind whenever they saw me, so I tried to refer to it at once so they didn't have to wonder if they should ask. I said, "Hi! I'm Karen. I had a car accident; that's why I look like this," so that they would be at ease and my appearance wouldn't be a barrier. My parents were absolutely devastated and became terribly protective trying to keep me in the house and away from anyone. Because my old friends were the unsuitable ones, I was soon back doing drugs and stuff with them. One of the good things that came out of my accident was that I was able to go to a computer programming training school for the disabled. My father weaseled me in, saying I was disabled. I don't think I was, but it was the best thing that ever happened to me. After that, I began working as a programmer.

During that time, I met someone named Susie, who had only recently moved to Connecticut and was the friend of a friend. She was an alcoholic and went into rehab, and six months later she was joined by her husband, Brian, who had stayed behind in their former home in Florida. We all became friends, and soon afterward Brian decided to leave Susie because she had started fooling around with quite a few men around the place. He divorced her and then moved away. Then, eight months later, he came back to town, and we met up again on the night I turned 21. He was 12 years older than me, but we started going out. Like Susie, he was an alcoholic and had been since he was 18.

I was living with my mom and dad, but Brian had no place to stay, so I let him live in my car. My mother hated him so much that she wouldn't even let him in the house. Then, when I was 22, I found out I was pregnant. My mom and dad were horrified, but after that they let Brian sleep on our back porch.

Our baby daughter, Kayla, was born, and Brian and I moved with her into a tiny apartment. Not long afterward, we all moved to New York state, where our second daughter, Sara, was born. Brian was drinking as much as ever. He was a drunk and he was mean and nasty. Although he never physically abused me, he yelled at me all the time, and I yelled at him all the time. We had all kinds of shouting matches. If Brian was not working, he was actively drinking. Sara was born three months premature, so a visiting nurse came out one day to check how she was doing. She looked at Sara and said, "Oh, she's absolutely fine."

Then suddenly she said, "How come Kayla's not walking right?"

I said, "What do you mean, Kayla's not walking right?"

I had noticed for some time that Kayla could not stand up from a sitting position without crawling over to the wall and kind of pulling herself up. I had taken her to a doctor who had said that she had low blood sugar. That was it.

But the nurse watched her walking and said, "Something's wrong with her." So they sent her for tests. At first they thought she might have cerebral palsy, then they came back and said it was muscular dystrophy. That was just horrible. It means she has some cells in her spine that don't fire correctly, so the stimulus from her brain doesn't get to her extremities correctly. It means that her muscles get weaker and weaker. It's a progressive, degenerative disease.

When they initially diagnosed her, they told her that she would be in a wheelchair by the time she was ten, and that she would probably be dead by the time she was 20. But she needed the wheelchair by the time she was seven. Nevertheless, I don't believe the whole 20 thing. She's in such good health, and I've heard from other doctors since that she should live much longer than that.

It was then that I started getting really mad at God. Not only was I dealing with an alcoholic husband and a three-month-premature baby, but now I heard my other daughter had muscular dystrophy. I was living in an isolated part of upstate New York, up in the mountains, with no car. I was 500 miles away from my mother and I knew nobody. Now, looking back on it, I don't know how I got through it. By now Brian was not even pretending to control his alcohol. When Kayla was diagnosed, his alcohol took on a whole new level. He started getting mad a lot more often, because he wasn't dealing with the anger he felt. It was just ugly, but I was so busy with the kids that I didn't have time to worry about him.

Despite all this, Brian and I got married in 1991, soon after Sara's birth. The reason was simply that it was getting very confusing using my maiden name at the doctor's. I said to Brian, "You need to marry me so that I can have the same name as you and the kids!"

We were married by a Justice of the Peace in New York. My mom and dad drove the five-hour journey from Connecticut to New York the night before. That night,

Brian decided that since he was getting married the next day, he'd better go out and get really drunk. He got so drunk, he could barely stand up. When he got home, he had a furious fight with my mother because of something to do with the air conditioning. It was the stupidest thing. It was only because he was drunk. So the two of them released all the anger they had held onto for years. They got so mad that my parents got into the car and left. So they didn't come to my wedding. I was not happy about that. I wasn't happy with Brian, but neither was I happy with my mother. She knew he was an alcoholic, so she could have been quiet when he started screaming at her.

In the end, we had just a few friends and no near family. We just had a little thing after. It was nice, but it would have been nicer if my mother had been there. Of course Brian was totally drunk through the day. During this time, Brian got arrested three times for DUI—driving while under the influence of alcohol.

So in 1994, when he was arrested the third time, he went to jail for a month and was then put into an alcoholic treatment center as part of his probation. He stayed there for six weeks and when he got home, he was sober for the next eight months. It was lovely—but not totally good because he was still mad all the time. He was so angry. He was what I call a "dry drunk." After eight months, he started drinking again, and that was when he started hiding his alcohol. But I knew. I could tell by his eyes. I could tell by his tone of voice. I could tell by his speech patterns. That was when he changed from drinking beer to vodka.

The next year, in 1995, I decided to put my resume on the internet, not thinking anyone would call me. But they did! Someone from Atlanta called me. So I talked to Brian and we decided to move to Atlanta. Then, one month before we were due to leave, Brian was arrested on another drunk driving charge and was sentenced to six months in jail. I said to him, "I cannot believe you did this." I was so mad. Anyway, while we were in court, we told the judge that we were leaving the state in 30 days and appealed to him to let Brian out in 30 days. We didn't know whether or not they would let us leave. In the end, they did. They let us leave.

So we moved to Georgia. Brian seemed to be mad all the time. Mostly he would be yelling at me, but I yelled back at him. I wasn't going to let him talk to me like that in front of my kids and not stick up for myself. I threatened to leave him, and it got so bad that I'd threaten him with that every single night. He got sick of hearing it. He tried giving up drinking, but he just couldn't. He had been an alcoholic for more than 30 years.

I had a friend at work, Lowell, who was a Christian. I remember telling him once, "You're such a good programmer. I wish I could be half the programmer you are."

He replied, "Karen, everything good I have comes from God. Everything bad I am comes from me."

I looked at him and laughed. I said, "You're crazy. What's wrong with you?" But I never forgot it. And I started watching him.

Around 1998, Brian collapsed in the parking lot and was

in a coma in intensive care for two months. Then he just magically woke up, and I thought, *There you go. You've got to stop drinking now.* He went to another rehab in Georgia and started taking those pills that make you throw up if you have a drink. They didn't help. He just kept drinking. For years he had said, "When I decide I want to stop, I'll be able to stop." But he couldn't. I found little bottles of vodka hidden underneath the couch, cushions, on top of the cabinet, in the back of the tomatoes, on the bottom of the refrigerator—everywhere, everywhere. It was horrible. By early 2001, things had gotten so bad that I had to take the girls and we'd have to leave. I didn't want to be in the house. He would scream and yell and punch holes in the wall. The girls would say, "Mom, we don't want to go home. Daddy's going to be drunk."

And I'd say, "Let's just go and see. Maybe he isn't today."

We'd go home, and he'd be drunk. I'd leave them in the car and go and check how drunk he was. If he was too drunk, we'd leave.

One day the girls said they wanted to go to church. They had friends at school who went, and my mom was into the New Age and other spiritual stuff, so they wanted to find out. I had been baptized Episcopalian, so we went to the nearest Episcopalian church (though we had never been). As we went in, we were handed the service sheet with a pamphlet advertising something called the Alpha course. We enjoyed the service and went back the following Sunday, when someone talked about the Alpha course from the front. I remember thinking, *Oh, that's exactly what I want to do.*

After we had been going for awhile, Kayla joined the choir. On the first Sunday that she was singing, Brian came, but he was not happy about it. A month later, I went to Alpha on the Sunday afternoon. Kayla and Sara came with me and went to the daycare, where they had fun helping to look after the younger children. There were about 60 people in the class, but I was part of a small group, and it was wonderful. I was very honest and said what I thought about being mad at God. Then I began to think, *How can I be mad at Him if He doesn't exist?* That night I asked one of the guys in my group, "Is there a good book I should be reading?" He suggested *Mere Christianity* by C. S. Lewis, so I went out and bought it. I had to call in sick to work the next day because I couldn't stop reading it. I read it twice in one day. I could not stop crying. It was a great book.

We continued going to church, and I heard about a healing service they held on Wednesday nights. One Wednesday, Brian was really drunk, and the girls and I were going to go to a hotel room. Then I remembered the Wednesday service, and I said, "We'll just sit in the back of the church. Nobody will notice us." There were only eight people and, as we talked, I told them about Brian being an alcoholic. So they all began praying for him, which was amazing.

After that, we kept going back on Wednesdays, and they prayed for Brian every time. Around the fourth or fifth week of the course, we had the class on "How and Why

Should I Read the Bible?" I was very proud of myself because I bought a Bible, and I went home to read it.

As I was reading it at home a couple of days later, I was smoking away, and I suddenly looked at my cigarette and thought, *Why am I doing this?* I had a whole wall of smoke all around me and I thought, *No wonder God can't reach you. He can't get through the smoke!* So I decided to quit smoking, and I haven't picked up a cigarette since. That was a big thing for me. Until then, I never went without a cigarette. I probably started smoking when I was about 13 or 14 and until that day—October 4, 2001—it had never even occurred to me to stop. That was a Wednesday, and that night we went to the healing service at church as usual. I mentioned that I hadn't had a cigarette that day and Kayla said, really quietly, "Mommy, you can't lie in church. Don't lie in church." She couldn't believe that I had stopped.

I wanted to share all that was happening to me with Brian, and one night we talked for quite a long time about the book *Mere Christianity*. But the next day he teased me unmercifully about it, saying, "You're stupid. What the heck you reading that junk for?"

I started praying, asking God, "You have to give me the strength to get through what I have to get through." But nothing seemed to be changing at home.

In late October, it all became too much for me, and I decided to throw Brian out. But I couldn't just abandon him. I love my husband. So I booked a hotel room and told Brian to go and live there. I made sure it was within walking distance of stores, and I got him some food for the refrigerator. I bought him a cell phone, so he could get in touch with me.

In the meantime, I continued to change. I suddenly stopped swearing. Everything used to be, "Oh, my God! Oh, Jesus Christ!" But now it didn't sound right, so I just quit saying those words. My Alpha group started praying for Brian too, which was lovely. So now I was praying for him on Sundays as well as Wednesdays. A few days after he went to the hotel, he called me on the telephone, and we had a long talk. Then he said, "You've got something now that I want, and I don't know how to get it." I told him it was God. Soon we were talking all night long, and he would be asking, "Well what about this" and "What about that?"

And I was saying, "Well, if you read this passage in the Bible . . ." I didn't know where these words were coming from. I'm not a preacher, but I was reading him all this stuff out of the Bible.

Then he said, "I'd like to go to church with you on Sunday." We met him in the parking lot at church. We were getting ready to go in and he suddenly said, "I'm not going; I'm leaving." And he left! I was crying. I was so mad.

That Tuesday night he called me again and was asking me more questions about God and Jesus. I said, "I can't answer any more. You're driving me crazy. Let me call my priest."

So I called Mary at church and she said, "Bring Brian in tomorrow morning." So I did. Wednesday morning we went to church. She and Brian and I got together. She listened to him and we prayed together. At that time, he had this huge cramp in his arm. And I said, "Look at that horrible cramp."

Mary put her hand on his arm, said a quick little prayer, and when he got out he said, "What did she do to me? I can feel this heat just radiating through my body."

The following Wednesday, he came to the healing service. The moment he walked in, they all gave him a big hug. He said, "Would you pray for me to know what to do?" So that is what we did. The next day, he called me in a terrible state and said, "My body's getting torn into pieces." He tried to contact Mary, but it was her day off. So I asked my work friend, Lowell, to call him. Lowell spoke to him for two hours. Brian said that as soon as he hung up the phone, he gave his life to God. He came to Christ and hasn't had anything to drink since! God took his thirst away instantly. There's no other way to explain it. I could tell the difference in him instantly. And he came back to live with us that Friday, November 3, 2001.

When I took him back, I took him back a different person. I took back my husband. So it was wonderful. The kids had a father, I had a husband, we had a family. Brian came to Alpha with us that Sunday, and they were all so pleased to see him. They had been praying for him for weeks. Now when we go to church on Sundays, Brian is the first out of the house. He says, "Will you hurry up? I want to get a good seat."

Brian and I now say the Lord's Prayer together every morning and every night. He has quit swearing and is reading the New Testament, which is amazing because I've never ever known him to read a book. In the evenings, we turn the TV off now and just talk. God has been wonderful to me. He's giving me strength and helps me through all this. And I think He is really guiding me and guiding Brian and the kids. Brian came to the final sessions of Alpha and then the celebration supper at the end. It was lovely, lovely.

For Christmas 2000, Brian and I spent way too much money, and the kids were all miserable. Brian was drunk. For Christmas 2001, we went to four services on Christmas Eve! We decided only to get each other one or two presents because it was Jesus' birthday. So I got both the girls crosses for Christmas and they loved them. We had a wonderful Christmas.

They don't get nervous about their father any more. They don't say, "Mom, we can't go home. Daddy's going to be drunk."

"He took my desire to drink away."

BRIAN'S STORY

I was born in 1953 and raised in a log cabin, way up in the mountains of Oregon. My father was an alcoholic lumberjack who beat my mother. It was a primitive lifestyle and most of the time we ate off a potbellied, wood-burning stove. My mother was very strong and put up with it for 13 years, but in the end she left. She couldn't take it no more.

Me and my brother and sister went with her. I was ten years old and I have never seen my father again.

My mom remarried a serviceman, and we ended up on the East Coast, and that's where I graduated from high school. It was the early 70s, and I got tied up bad with drugs and alcohol. In the early days, I only took drugs. If I took drugs—and a bit of wine—I didn't feel like alcohol. I didn't want it because I said I'd never grow up and be like my dad. I quit all my drugs by my mid-twenties, but the alcohol just kept multiplying. However much I quit the drugs, the one that always stayed was alcohol.

I have done lots of jobs. My favorite job of all time was when I worked the riverboats, pushing barges from Houston, Texas, up the Mississippi River to Pittsburgh and then back. It would take 30 days to make a trip. It was a single man's paradise, because you stay on the boat 30 days, couldn't spend no money, and when you got off you had a pocketful of money with another 30 days to do what you wanted. My life was just drinking and "cutting up"—laughing and playing guitars. And I always kept women around.

When I was 27, I got married, but it only lasted two years. I would work, and then we'd get drunk. That was our life. If I wasn't working or sleeping, I was drinking. Suzie had a drug habit and would have sex with other men. In the end, I said, "That's it. I'm leaving."

Karen and I started out as friends. I was homeless for a while and slept in her car. The friendship grew into a bond, which turned out to be beautiful. When Karen told me she was pregnant, I was drug running with a friend, who was a dealer. It was just cocaine. I said to Karen, "Are you sure?" She said yes, and we decided to go with it. At the time, I was drinking a lot with this male friend. Our breakfast was what we called "bacon and eggs." Bacon was Budweiser and eggs was cocaine. That's how we started at five o'clock each morning.

When Karen and I moved to New York, I gave up the drugs, but I was still drinking as much as I could drink. I don't know how Karen put up with me passing out every night. When Kayla was diagnosed with her illness, I cursed and screamed inside. I was totally destroyed. I broke many knuckles on walls and trees.

I was also angry because my drinking was totally out of control, and there was nothing I could do. I couldn't do anything with my alcoholism, I knew that. Even when I managed to stop drinking through A.A., I was still a drunk who wasn't drinking. I was trying to be good and do good. I remember the day I popped open a little miniature bottle of vodka. Not long afterward I was drinking a half pint of vodka in three gulps. It reminded me of my heroin fix because it was so quick. Then I'd get more and get more and that's when I would black out. By the end, I was drinking half a gallon of vodka a day. Thank God, He gave me a very, very strong body.

Then Karen started going to that church. I didn't mind. I was pleased for her. But I knew when she was praying for me. I asked her one morning, "Have you all been praying for me?"

She said, "Yes."

I said, "Quit it! You're making me miserable. I'm losing my mind over this."

After a while, Karen began getting softer and softer to the point of saying, "I've had enough." One day she said, "Brian, I've had enough. We are not going to take this no more." I didn't argue. I had lost. I gave up my job and everything. I thought I might take off with my old biker buddies from the days when I used to ride a Harley Davidson. But the change in Karen was obvious. It was like night and day. She never used to talk to people unless she knew them very well. The car wreck which disfigured her face had major implications to her whole life. But now you could see the joy and happiness in her.

We were sitting in a waffle house, and I remember looking at her and saying, "I want that peace in me." I could see the love. We were both full of tears, and I said, "Now we can't have two Whaleys weeping in a waffle house—come on now."

I thought Mary, the priest Karen took me to, was wonderful. She is so spiritually gifted. It just drips off her.

Then, the next day, I spoke with Lowell. I didn't trust him. Being a biker, druggie, drunk, I don't trust a man around my woman like that. But I came to find out he is so innocent. He's been a Christian his whole life. That night, we finally had a good talk. At one point, we talked about fishing, and he said, "You know, Brian, we could be friends."

That Thursday night is when I gave myself to the Lord. It was four in the morning, and I remember sitting in a chair looking out of the window and asking Jesus to take over. I asked Him to help me stop drinking. I just said, "Take it away." The next thing I knew I woke up. I was on the verge of blacking out when I asked Him in. I was pretty drunk. When I woke up, I was a different person. As soon as I woke up, I knew. I had no thirst for alcohol. My whole inner being was different; I wasn't worried any more.

Then, the following Sunday, I went to Alpha, and they were all hugging me. I didn't know none of them, but they said, "Look at him. He's here, he's here." They were all so pleased. I have quit cursing too. Once in a while I'll get very frustrated and a curse word will pop out and I'll say, "Whoops!" It's just unbelievable.

Now I pray all the time. I'm in walking prayer. I say, "Praise You and thank You, Jesus," all the time. I've never liked reading before. I don't read. The only time I ever read was when I was incarcerated in jail for a few days or a few weeks or a few months. Now I've read all the New Testament. And I go back and start reading it again, because you get different things at different times.

As for the family, we've always loved each other, but now the kids aren't scared of me. I used to get so drunk that I couldn't see the fear in the children. They used to go into the bedroom and stay there when I was drunk, which was every night. It would make me cry sometimes. I'd try to sleep because they were so afraid of me. It was that bad. But Karen has told me that when I went out to the store the other day, Kayla said to her, "Isn't it wonderful?"

Karen said, "What?"

"That Daddy can go to the store and come home again and he won't be drunk."

Karen and Brian Whaley attend St. Peter and St. Paul's Episcopal Church, Marietta, Georgia, and participate in many church activities. They help with church Alpha courses.

"I went to jail when I was five months pregnant. I was in a room with two other women, but I felt so alone. You could sit there and cry and people would walk right by you. They didn't care. Everybody was crying."

8

THE STORY OF PAULA CAPRIOTTI

Paula Capriotti of Philadelphia, lived a life dominated by her compulsive drug habit. She served a prison sentence but found it impossible to stay clear of drugs on her release. With her life falling apart, a friend stepped in to help.

I am the youngest of five. I have three older brothers and my one sister, who is 19 years older than me. My brother closest in age to me is 11 years older. I was kind of a surprise child. My father was an alcoholic, and it got to be really a burden on the family. There was a lot of fighting at home. He used to display a lot of anger, but he never hit me. Mom used to take us to the local Catholic church, and I made it through 12 years of Catholic school. But I started smoking marijuana at about 12, and by about 14 I was using chemicals—like cocaine and pills.

One of the reasons I went toward drugs was that I couldn't stand alcohol because of what it did to my dad. Mom and dad caught us smoking pot once, and the cops came to the house, but it wasn't a big deal to her because all my brothers smoked pot. By the time I graduated from school, my dad and my brother were both in jail. One of my brothers who was a drug addict had been in and out of jail since I was seven. He was now 18. He would rob houses and steal jewelry and money for drugs. My dad had also been drinking and driving, and she had him locked up. I can remember the house being nice and peaceful. But when dad came out, I could not bear to be in that environment, so I went to live with another of my brothers.

I was on drugs all this time and used to sell drugs to pay for them. When I was about 21, I got my own apartment and went to college, where I got good grades. At that time I started drinking too, and I would get really drunk. Then I would snort coke, smoke pot, and end up puking my guts out. I remember thinking, "Oh gosh, I hope I don't do this again tonight." Then I'd eat something and go to work . . . and by the time I got off work, I would be ready to go back out again. I did that for at least three years. I had no other life except for work (I worked as a cook) and drink and party and sleep for all that time. I was so unhappy that I would cry myself to sleep at night, but I didn't stop.

That was when I started smoking crack, and it really started swirling down the tubes. I became really, really depressed. You feel like a rat on a wheel. The highs are very short, and you keep wanting more and more. It does something to your brain and makes you totally paranoid. You don't trust anyone, and it gives you a horrible feeling. But, horrible as it feels, you want more, and all you care about is having more. You can stare out of the window for an hour and think there's somebody out there, but there's no one there. I have heard of people peeking under doors and wearing carpet burns into their face from just looking under the door.

My boyfriend wasn't enslaved to it as much as I was. He would keep me on a string with the drugs, throwing me a little bit of drugs, then going out for the night. I stole from him almost every night toward the end. I stole from his change, his cameras, his jewelry, leather coats—anything I could.

Eventually, in August of 1995, I told the woman I worked for that I was really bad on drugs, and she took me to a rehab and I remained a patient there for 30 days. When it was over, all I was thinking about was when I was going to get high again. My boyfriend came to pick me up at six o'clock the morning of the day I was supposed to be discharged. The next day I asked him for some money to get a hair cut, and I went and bought some drugs. At the same time I took some money out of my mom's bank account.

She had the same name as me, so I went to her bank, took some money out, and got a hotel room and a whole bunch of crack.

I called my boyfriend from the room and told him where I was, because I was freaking out. He came and got me. He took me home and was really mad at me, because he thought I was going to get my act together. I was just crying. After that he became like a cop, searching me and following me. He even pulled all the wires out of my car because I was using it to go and buy drugs. It was driving me crazy, and I hated him for it.

"Just leave me alone and let me get high," I said to him.

Finally, one day, he said, "Go with your junkie friends and get out. Go live with your brother."

My brother was out of jail at the time, and I went to stay with him. He fixed my car and we went to this other guy's house to do drugs. At one point the guy asked me to take some drugs to another place, and he would give me some in return. When I got back, the cops busted in the house and locked us all up. It was a set-up. That was two weeks after I got out of the rehab—October 4, 1995. They kept me in jail—Delaware County Prison—for a couple of nights after which my mom put up a twenty-five thousand dollar cash bail, putting up her house to do it. They sentenced me to between 11 and 23 months.

Just before I got sentenced, I found out I was pregnant. The baby must have been conceived during the two weeks I was out of rehab. I honestly don't know how it happened because all I did for those two weeks was get high. So here

I was, smoking crack, doing acid, and drinking alcohol—and I was pregnant with a little girl.

I went to jail when I was five months pregnant on March 1, 1996. I was in a room with two other women, but I felt so alone. Everybody else felt the same. You could sit there and cry and people would walk right by you. They didn't care. Everybody was crying. We were all in the same boat. On the first Sunday I went to church, and I couldn't even sit through the worship, because my heart was breaking out of my chest. It hurt so bad, I just wanted to cry. I remember wanting to leave the service but I couldn't. I was immobilized. I couldn't even move. I made friends with a woman who would come in and pray on my stomach for my baby. I prayed with her to ask God into my life, but I don't think I realized what I was praying.

I was released from prison on July 2—two months in advance. I had a good lawyer who had it written into my sentence that I would get out, have the baby, stay home with the baby for two months, then come back and finish my sentence. The baby, named Natalie Rose, was born four days after my release. I took her home to my mom. In the second week of August, I relapsed and started doing drugs again. I left Natalie by herself to go and get them. I left her in the crib, and I could barely forgive myself after I had done that. I wasn't gone long, but anything could have happened to me. I could have gotten locked up; I could have gotten killed or in a car accident and never come back. Anything could have happened, but I did make it back. It was just such foolishness. The power of the drugs takes away your maternal instinct.

In September they took me back for re-sentencing. I was then put on parole and given a leg monitor to ensure they could watch where I went. I was still doing drugs, but in the second week of January, I did something crazy. I was in and out of the house all night long doing drugs. When I got home in the morning, my mom was freaking out—and I started doing the same. I knew that I was going to go back to jail. One Friday night at five o'clock, the cops came and locked me up in front of my mom and my baby. I went back to jail and had to leave my baby at home. I cried for two weeks. I had violated my parole, and they could have kept me up until the two years they had sentenced me to in the beginning.

One Sunday a woman from a local church came to the prison, and I met and talked to her. Her name was Karen Meiklejohn. She sat down next to me, and I poured tears and begged her to help me. I told her my baby was at home and that if I didn't get help, I was going to die. She wrote to me, and ten days later, they sentenced me to a half-way house. They would let me out on Sundays to go to work, but instead I would go to the Covenant Fellowship Church with my baby to meet Karen. That happened throughout the three months I was in the half-way house.

I got out in April 1997. That July I decided I wanted to go out with my friends. I went to a club and I was dancing and stuff, but I didn't drink. A week later I went back to the club and I drank. Later that night I was out doing drugs again. Toward the end of August I was back to doing it every day, and my whole motivation was crack. I was just consumed with thoughts of doing crack. I was still on parole and knew I was going to end up in jail again. I couldn't bear the thought of leaving my baby again, so I called this rehab place and told them what was going on. They put me in an intensive outpatient program every day in the afternoon from about 5 till 7 at night. But I still relapsed in there. I would sit there and cry, saying, "How can all you people sit here and tell me you do not want to get high?" During this time, I had stopped going to church, but Karen kept writing to me and calling me.

Then, on the night of October 12, 1997, I lay in bed and looked at my hands. I knew that my flesh had power over me and that I needed God's power to triumph over it. So I prayed for God to help me. I told Him I was completely incapable of stopping on my own and that I was totally enslaved to my flesh and what my flesh wanted. The next day I went back to see Karen at the church. I managed to stay clean and a short while later, Karen and her husband Will told me about a course called Alpha which was starting at the church in January.

They said, "You really should go."

And I said, "I'm there."

It was held in the home of a couple of church members named Dana and Seva who seemed so Christian, so perfect, so far out of my reach, that I could not see them ever being my friends. There were 14 people there and Jim, the pastor, was the leader. I was the only crack addict, and I felt a total outsider. It was the first time they had ever put on the course at that church. The supper was great and I loved the dessert. I used to look forward to that and each week would ask, "What's for dessert?" We watched the talks on video and at first I found the English accent of Nicky Gumbel, the presenter, hard to understand, but gradually I understood it more and got used to it.

As the weeks went by, I really enjoyed the course and would finish each evening so juiced up. I just loved it. At home, I couldn't wait to put the baby to bed at night, because that would be my time to read books from the church and to pray.

A month into the course, I went to see my dad, who is an alcoholic, to tell him that I loved him and that I understood why he had acted in the way he did toward us when we were children. At that stage he was in and out of the hospital because his organs had deteriorated so much. I told him that Jesus was helping me to stop doing what I was doing. Soon afterward, they put him in a nursing home, and I prayed with him and tried to read the Bible to him.

On the night he fell into a coma, I was with him, and I sat there thinking about how God had protected me all through my times on drugs where I was in terrible situations—and now He had put me in a place where I could be with my dying dad and reach out to him. As I sat there, I said, "Lord, I am Yours forever, and I want to walk with You forever. I want to do Your work. I want to serve You." I gave Him my life right then and there. I was all by myself, and the tears came so strongly that I thought I had flipped. The next day we buried him. We had a service. Lots of people from the church, including the leader from my Alpha group, came to my dad's funeral on the Wednesday before the Alpha retreat.

On the day the retreat began, that Friday, as I drove my car to work that day, I was looking for a match in the car, when I found this big bag of drugs under the seat—and I had it in my hand. I sat looking at it and I thought, *If I do these drugs, I'm never going to make it to the retreat.* I had been clean at that time for four months. Suddenly I said, "No, I'm not doing them," and I threw them away as far as I could. I was crying and I remember saying, "Somebody, please come." Then my boss pulled up in her car. I told her what had happened, and she dumped the bag.

That night I went on the retreat and had a great weekend. After Alpha, I got plugged into the Covenant Fellowship Church, and the people there really served me. I joined a small group where I cried all the time. Jesus is now my light and my joy. He's always there, He's always working, and He's always revealing something. I seem to be praying to Him all the time now. I never saw how much I was sinning before. I knew that doing drugs was a sin, but now so many more sins are revealed, and I need Him so much more.

Now I trust God for my future. I can't see myself going back to drugs now, though there is still a lot of temptation. After coming to know Jesus and getting clean it seemed like the sun shone for like a year. It never rained. The sky was always blue. The birds were always singing. Everything seemed so beautiful.

I would look back to my old life and had some nostalgia, but then I'd know that God was saying, "What are you looking back for? I have good plans for you up ahead, over this mountain. Just trust Me."

I know now that I am truly forgiven. Believing in Jesus Christ has given me peace in my heart, a hope, and a future. He has placed my feet on the rock and made my path straight.

In February 2001, Paula Capriotti married Michael Kyle, whom she met at church. They had a little girl named Talitha Grace, on March 13, 2002. Paula says, "I can't express all of my gratitude to God for all He has done in my life."

"On a general day I would have three or four martinis at lunch and then four to six after work. Then I would go home and drink by myself."

THE STORY OF MICHAEL KYLE

After a life blighted by drink and drugs, Michael Kyle of Philadelphia, saw his successful hairdressing business run into crisis. He became seriously depressed and wanted to die. Then one of his clients handed him an envelope.

I grew up in a loving home, but my father wasn't around a lot. He worked a lot, and when he wasn't working, he was mostly at the bar. His absence caused a lot of stress on the marriage. I was partying at other people's houses from about tenth grade (15 years old). I was drinking, smoking pot, doing drugs. I eventually sold drugs—marijuana, LSD, angel dust. But my dad kept a lid on my partying, because he was a big man and carried a big stick.

My dad died when I was about 20, and it was a real shock. I had just started working for him, and I had begun having a real relationship with him. But when he died, my brother and I both left the company. I then trained as a hairdresser—but my partying got a whole lot worse. I would get up in the morning and get high. I would smoke pot or angel dust and then go to school. At lunch and after work, I would drink vodka, beer—anything. I was going to a psychiatrist, taking anti-depressants, and mood elevators. At night I would go and shoplift Nyquil to get to sleep. It was a really insane existence, and it lasted for nine years. I would get up in the morning, and basically, stick my finger down my throat. Toward the end I would just throw up blood. The only time I really started feeling better was when I started drinking. I had a couple of doctors on the hook for my anti-depressant pills, so I could get double prescriptions from a couple of pharmacies.

When I was 28, I became very sick and just crashed. There wasn't a particular event that brought it on. It was just that I'd had enough. I was tired of being sick. I just really wanted someone to stop me. By that time, I could easily finish off a bottle of vodka or gin a day. Pot had started to make me paranoid, so I didn't really like it anymore. On a general day I would have three or four martinis at lunch and then four to six after work. Then I would go home and drink by myself. That's how you end up. So what I did was to go to a doctor and told him that I wasn't sleeping and that I was throwing up. He did a series of tests and then said, "I don't know what's the matter with you. Everything appears fine; you're fit as a fiddle."

I couldn't believe what I was hearing! I said, "Do you think this could be caused by drinking too much?"

"Are you drinking too much?" he asked.

"Yeah, I think so."

He wrote out a prescription to Eagleville Rehabilitation

Center. It was actually a converted tuberculosis hospital, so they had been around some time. It was one of the rougher places. You couldn't fool anybody there. I did a 17-day program in the rehab—an accelerated program for employed people. I was very shaky, very sick, and I didn't sleep for days. When you drink yourself to sleep every night for years and years, your body shuts down its own ability to go to sleep. It was a very unpleasant time. I sweated so badly that my hands literally peeled. I sat there with a towel all day wiping my palms. I came out sober and started going to Alcoholics Anonymous and Narcotics Anonymous. I never drank or took drugs again.

In 1990 I opened my own salon in Havertown, and it was very successful. Three years later I got married, and our son, Billy, was born in January, 1995. My wife and I divorced when he was only six months old. That was a bad time, but I was never tempted to go back to drinking. We arranged that I would have Billy for four nights each week.

In January of 1997 the entire salon staff quit in one day. They conspired together and took all their customers to a new shop one of them was starting down the street. It was terrible. Four cutters went all at once. I was probably a bad boss—cranky and unreasonable—but I was left ten-thousand dollars in debt and had to take twenty-six thousand out of my individual retirement just to stay in business. I was seriously, seriously depressed. I wouldn't say that I wanted to kill myself, but I wanted to die.

Soon afterward, I moved in with a girl who was really young (I was 40; she was 26), but that Christmas it ended suddenly. We knew we weren't in love. It was just not ever going to move forward. We weren't enemies at all. But for me that was the breaking point.

About a year before this, one of my clients, Jill Vanderweid, had given me a letter with two tapes inside. I knew she was a Christian because she had in the past said things like, "Jesus is who you really need." I had just thought, *Yeah, yeah. This is crazy.* Anyway, she had dropped this letter off at the shop, and I had never opened it. It would just sit on my bureau, and when this all happened, I walked upstairs one day and opened it.

It was very, very well written and described a biblical view of God's perspective on my life. I was impressed by the fact that it was hand-typed, not word-processer-typed. I read the letter, listened to the tapes, and remember thinking, *I think I am going to go to church.* On my way to work later that day I thought, *I really need to call Jill and thank her for writing that letter and tell her that I am going to come to church.* I walked into the bank and suddenly, there she was! I said, "What are you doing here?"

She said, "Oh, I never usually come to the bank, but Brian [her husband] called me specifically to ask me to come in."

I said, "It's funny because I was going to call you this morning."

I apologized to her for not having read the letter. And then I thanked her and told her I was coming to church that Sunday to the Covenant Fellowship Church. I came to the church for a few weeks and then—this was March of

1998—there was a service when a girl spoke about her experiences on something called the Alpha course. I can't remember what she said. There was nothing similar about her story to mine. She had children and she was divorced, and that was about it. But I just knew that I needed to go, so I went to Jill and said, "I am going to go to Alpha."

A few weeks later, I pulled up outside a home with balloons going up the walkway. I walked in, and about ten people were there. We had supper, then they put on the video. I was tired, but I enjoyed it. I came back because in the group time afterward, they were willing to pay attention to me and listen to me. I didn't really have many friends. I began to look forward to Thursday nights.

About the sixth week we went on a retreat at Black Rock Retreat Center in Lancaster. On the Friday night the pastor, Jim Donohue, spoke on the holiness of God. I roomed with John, my small group leader, and we stayed up most of the night talking about God and the Bible. After the Saturday morning meeting, Jim invited anyone who wanted to come up front to receive Christ as their personal Savior. I was the first one up there. I confessed my sin to God, asked Him to forgive me through His Son's death on the cross, and I accepted Jesus Christ as my personal Lord and Savior.

The next morning—May 30, 1998—I went to church, and the worship started. They sang a song called *Covenant of Grace*. In the song there is a line which says, "...and welcome you to this place." At that, I began sobbing. I was literally undone on the spot. I was uncontrollably sobbing for the whole service practically, and that morning I was radically transformed. It was the most unbelievable thing that I have ever experienced in my life. It was like when the movie, *The Wizard of Oz,* changes from black and white to color. That's what happened. All of a sudden my eyes were opened, and I saw and experienced God in my life. I had a desire to read the Bible, and when I opened it, I understood it.

I started attending a care group where I met a single mom named Paula Capriotti. We were baptized the same night, we dedicated our children to God the same day, and she lived just a few blocks away. We eventually married on February 3, 2001 and were blessed with a baby girl named Talitha Grace Kyle, born on March 13, 2002.

Today I try to serve God with all my strength, heart, and mind, and seek His will for my family. Today Jesus is my brother and my friend. He is my Savior, my Lord, and my reason for living. I can't stop thanking Him!

Michael Kyle now leads worship in his church small group and teaches primary school children once a month on Sunday mornings. He says, "I could go on and on telling you about all God's blessings to me and my family."

*"I thought, This is it. This is rock bottom. I'm getting messed up
with the wrong people."*

9

THE STORY OF LISA BOEKE

*In her twenties,
Lisa Boeke lived
a promiscuous
lifestyle with much
drinking and way-
ward living. She
became intrigued
by New Age philos-
ophy and saw
everything as "just a learning experience." After marrying and having two daughters, she was invited to a
local church.*

I was brought up in Spirit Lake, Iowa, and have five brothers and sisters. Though we went to church, we didn't discuss things much. It was more liturgical.

When I was aged 10 or 11, my second brother became a Mormon. It was a time when things weren't going very well with his life. Then in 1971 my sister, Debra, ran away from home and went to California where she became a New Age follower. All this was hard for my mom and dad.

I did well when I was in school. I was fourth in my class and was a person who always did what I was supposed to do. But when I got into college, I went in completely the opposite direction. I stopped doing the things that I was best at, like music, and I started doing things that I should not have, like drinking, partying, and all that stuff. I led a promiscuous lifestyle and did a lot of things that I am not very proud of now.

I was at a very impressionable stage, and my sister Deb got me thinking about the whole New Age thing—and that's the direction in which I went for the next 17 years. I figured that Jesus was a wonderful person and did a wonderful thing, but to me He was one of many of God's prophets or "master teachers" on the earth.

Deb gave me a book called *I am Ramtha* about something called channeling. There was a woman by the name of J. Z. Knight who channeled this old being called Ramtha through her. She would go into a trance and speak about Ramtha, saying what seemed to be really wonderful things to people.

It talked about the fact that there was no heaven or hell, no good or bad, but that everything is just a learning experience. I thought, *Well, that makes sense.* It made life easier because "sins" suddenly did not exist anymore. Anything that you do is OK, and it doesn't matter how many times you do it, because it is a learning experience and eventually you'll get there. Basically, the idea is that no matter what you do, it's OK because eventually you are going to reach God. It might take you a number of lifetimes to get there, however. The teaching is that when you die, you come back in the same state somewhere else in the world. There is a lot of reincarnation involved. Deb sent me books and tapes and, most recently, a tape on conversations with God.

During the 1980s I drank a lot so I don't remember much. I drank every night when I was in college and became really good at it. I never became an alcoholic, but I could drink fast, so I would win "chug-off" contests to drink beer as fast as you can. I was real good at opening my throat, and the beer would fall down. I could down 12 ounces in about four seconds.

I graduated in 1986 (at least that's what my diploma says!) and I left college. I just got a Liberal Arts degree. My mom contracted cancer when I was at college, and when I moved back to Spirit Lake, my intention was to help out, but I didn't get along with my dad and things were stressful with my mom being sick. She had one good year after she went through her treatment, but then she died a horrible death.

After she died I was running in the rain, and I was beside myself with grief. I was alone and very upset. Then I felt a presence with me strongly at that moment, right beside me. It was a very comforting feeling at the time. It was really weird, but I still remember it clearly. At the time

I thought it was the presence of my mother. As I was running, I stopped and fell down with my head in my hands and said, "Mom, I'm going to miss you so much." At that moment it was almost as if I could feel someone hugging me. Now I believe it was God.

In 1987 I moved to Arizona to work for an insurance company, then I moved back to Iowa to be with a man I thought I wanted to marry. But it didn't work out. We had a long distance relationship for two years then lived together for three years, but we separated in 1994. I went through a depression at that time and really felt that life was just not worth living. I even considered suicide. Nothing was going the way it was supposed to, and I had no faith or anything at that point in time.

My sisters talked a lot about New Age philosophy, and Deb sent me some "medicine cards." They are like tarot cards with animals on them. You count them out and then after a certain number you pick a card and that's the animal that you are. It then talks about your inner spirits and your attributes related to that animal. I took it seriously. I continued to fall deeper into depression, and finally I saw a psychiatrist and was on Prozac for a while.

My thirty-second birthday was the low point of my life. My roommate introduced me to this guy friend of hers. I almost had a thing with him, and then I realized he was almost a schizophrenic, telling me a whole bunch of lies. I thought, *This is it. This is rock bottom. I'm getting messed up with the wrong people.* It makes me sick to think about it now.

I owned a house in Iowa City, and I sold it and bought a house in Spirit Lake. I worked for my brother-in-law, managing his office for a short time, and then I met my husband Gregg in 1994. I became pregnant in September, and we were married in December, 1994. I moved to Minneapolis in November of 1994 and our baby daughter, Kerri, was born in June.

Gregg is a wonderful guy. He was brought up in a Lutheran church like me, and his mother works for the ELCA Foundation of the Lutheran Church. His grandfather is a devoted Christian and is a wonderful man. It was important to Gregg that the children were raised in the church and Kerri was baptized in a Lutheran church nearby. We joined that church so we would have a church to belong to. Though I did not have a Christian belief anymore, it mattered to him. During the baptism classes, I asked questions like, "Why do you have to be baptized? Why did Jesus care if you put water on the baby's head?" I also took a Bible class because I thought it was time for me to figure out what the Bible was actually saying. I quit after the first two classes. There were just eight or nine people, and I couldn't get into what the leader was saying.

After a while we stopped going to the church. I just couldn't get my heart into it. Then my neighbor across the street invited me to these really huge Easter and Christmas programs at Hosanna Lutheran Church, which was closer to where we lived. Both my neighbor and my daycare provider were going. Their husbands wouldn't go to church, so I would go with them.

145

At first I couldn't stand it because it was so progressive and contemporary, and I was raised in a church that was so Lutheran and traditional, with jello and pot-luck suppers on Thursday nights after Lent. The service I was used to had organ music, liturgy, first lesson, second lesson, the Epistle and then the Gospel, the sermon, and then you had prayers. At this church all the music was on the big screen and they had a band. I thought, *Oh, yuck,* and then when people clapped and cheered it just killed me! I thought, *This is not church.* There would be tons of people — at least 500. The times I went it was always full. They were always happy to see new faces come in the door, but it's a big church, and you always feel kind of out of place.

In a church bulletin they were talking about the Alpha course. It said, "Do you think that life is all that it can be for you? Do you feel that you are missing out on something? You wonder why other people seem happier than you?" I thought, *Well, I do wonder. Everyone seems generally happy in here.* So I went to the course, and there were about 280 people there. At first, I was a little intimidated. I would ask questions like, "I don't understand how God can hold against the Jews their religion." I asked a whole lot of others, and nobody seemed really to know the answers. I thought I had stumped them all. Then my small group helper, Bob Sjoquist, gave me a book called *Searching Issues.* I started reading it, and it made so much sense and answered so many of my questions.

I kept going to the course because I liked the people and the way it was set up. Sitting down and having dinner is a great idea, and I've got two kids so it was nice to get out of the house for three hours. Pastor Dave was funny and really got his point across, while my small group was wonderful, with people who really cared about me. As time went on I found out that I was enjoying it more. I like to talk about things, and religion is an interesting thing to talk about.

Then the weekend came. I had never heard anything about the Holy Spirit in my entire life, but during that time I gave to God all the things that I had on my chest, and it was such a wonderful process. I was crying so hard when Pastor Dave was talking. Then he said, "Let yourself go. Close your eyes. Just pretend that you see Jesus in front of you. He is asking you to lean on Him and to give up everything on your heart." I did that, and I was so close to Jesus at that point in time, I immediately went up and really accepted Christ for the first time in my life. That was in January, 1999.

I always did everything that was expected of me until I got to be older. Then I didn't do anything that was expected of me, and my life really screwed up.

I think I've changed all of my thought processes since then. I really love to go to church and to become involved. I think of Jesus completely different now. I talk to Him now. Beforehand, I might have talked to the sky or to the universe in general. But now I actually feel like I am speaking to God the Father, God the Son—and He's listening, especially when I give Him the best time of my day in the morning. Now I read the Bible every day and I pray. For my whole life I have had a picture of Jesus knocking at the door and now, for the first time in my life, it means something to me.

I still feel like a baby Christian in so many ways. There are so many things I have to learn. I really believe that I am getting to know God a lot. I feel that He's in my life. Actually, I don't feel like He ever left me. I know I left Him.

Lisa and Gregg Boeke are still active members of Hosanna Lutheran Church. Gregg, inspired by Lisa's new-found faith, has become active in mission work, traveling to both Guatemala and Mexico. They now have three children (Kerri (7), Bridgett (3), and Simon (15 months). Lisa says, "We've been through some difficult times, but we know that God is leading us and that He will never abandon us."

> *"Suddenly my whole life was revealed to be a glass house which shattered and collapsed."*

THE STORY OF MARIE JOSEPH

Marie Joseph was devastated when her husband revealed to her that he was homosexual and that he would be leaving her and their three-year-old daughter and one-year-old son. Three years later, in her local Catholic church, she noticed a leaflet about the Alpha course.

I come from an Italian–Spanish home on Long Island and was brought up Catholic, though we didn't go to church regularly. I went to Cornell University where I had a boyfriend named Jim. We married in 1989, when I was 24 and he was 26. Everybody thought that we were a great, great couple and our wedding was a very happy occasion.

He was also a Catholic, and we married in a Catholic church in New York. We married in church because that was what you were supposed to do. Girls grow up with the dream of a wedding in a church and that's what we had. Jim also worked in marketing, and to start with we lived in

New York. Then we decided we wanted a better life and moved down to Yardley, Pennsylvania.

Our first child, Alicia, was born in 1993 and then, a year and a half later, we had a boy—JP, for James Patrick. I quit my job to stay home and be a full time mom. Jim was doing well, and we didn't mind losing the one salary, because we just wanted to live on less and have the quality of life. We kept making it our goal to have a good family life. We didn't have any particular faith in God, but we baptized the children. After that, we went to the local church occasionally but never on a regular basis, and it gradually trailed off. As the months passed, life started to feel a little harder, and I started to feel like I was missing something. I began to sense that Jim was feeling that way too. I didn't know what it was, but I started feeling some anger and resentment toward Jim. We did a bit of counseling and talked, but we couldn't determine what the problem was.

Finally, on August 22, 1996, I just sat him down and said something like, "Now what's really going on here?"

He said, "I want to tell you, but I'm not really sure, and I don't know if I will be able to take it back."

And at that moment a thought came to me. I suddenly said, "You are a homosexual, aren't you?"

And he said, "Yes."

We loved each other so much, that at that moment we embraced and held each other. Then I said, "I love you so much, I'm going to let you go. I don't want you to live a lie."

Suddenly my whole life, which was built around my husband, our two children, and our home, was revealed to be a glass house which shattered and collapsed. I experienced such pain. While my heart was just ripped apart, I also loved him and wanted him to be happy. He had never told anyone before me; he wasn't even really sure in his own mind. So it became a secret between us for a while. I couldn't even tell my family. In the end, I said, "Can I go tell a priest?"

And he said, "Yes, I'll let you tell a priest."

So I went to our big Catholic church—which I certainly did not perceive to be a warm, friendly, cozy kind of place—and, with hysterical crying, I told this priest. In the end, he said, "We need to pray for your husband."

And I said, "No, no, you don't understand. We're getting divorced. I love him and I'm letting him go. I'm here for me. What should I do? I don't feel like this is my thing. I don't know how to pray. I don't know anything about God."

He was a new priest, and he just said, "No, you don't understand. We need to pray for your husband." He said something about him being "healed."

I said, "You're nuts. I'm out of here. You obviously can't help me." I left and swore I would never go back.

Jim moved out on September 15, 1996. He found an apartment near our home in Yardley. The children were ages three and one. Before he moved out, I invited his mom and dad and other members of his family to the house and told them what had happened. Jim wasn't there. It seemed he didn't have the courage to be there. We all just sat and cried after I had told them the news. We agreed to love and support Jim throughout all this. I told my own parents on another occasion.

After Jim had moved out, I said to myself, *Well, I'm not going to church on Sunday mornings, but I need to go somewhere, so instead I will go to the gym and work out.* I had always had a problem with being overweight and over-eating and had a history of dieting, then eating, then dieting. My weight used to go up and down about 40 pounds a year. Over the years, it had ranged from 120 lbs. to 220 lbs. In 1993, I had lost 90 lbs. through healthy lifestyle changes—eating low-fat food and exercising. I had even started a little business helping women with dieting through exercise at home in a positive, nurturing, loving way. Instead of going to the gym and being harsh to your body, I tried to do it in a different way. So I went to the gym and trained to be an instructor.

Jim had a few boyfriends over the years, and I had relationships of my own. I used to go to parties and meet people, but they never lasted more than a couple of months. Then, on July 6, 1999, I said to myself, *I just can't do this anymore.* I had time to myself because Jim had taken the children away for a week, and I was alone and depressed. I went to a local bar at "Happy Hour" and started hanging around people who were drinking and smoking. I had never smoked before, but I started smoking that week.

At the end of the week I was sitting alone on my back deck in a lounge chair with a case of beer and a pack of cigarettes, smoking and drinking. And all of a sudden I looked around me, and it was all beautiful. The sun was out and the trees were beautiful. I didn't feel like I really knew God, but I said a kind of prayer. I just said, "You know, God, it's so beautiful what You have created. How can it be so beautiful out there and so horrible in here?" I said, "Is this how it's all going to end? Is this it? Is this all there is?"

And then, I had this feeling which just said, "No." So I got up and threw all the beer and cigarettes away. I trashed them all in my garbage pail, got up, and went to sleep. I woke up early the next morning and I thought, *Go to church.*

For around three years I had been bad-mouthing that priest who I had spoken to in 1996 and had looked around at different types of churches. But this time I went back to that big, cold, Catholic church. I went to the 7 a.m. mass, and I started listening to the words. I had never owned a Bible or said a prayer from my heart in my whole life. But the words I heard from the Bible that day sounded like hope. I thought, *Ooh, I want some of that.* During the prayer time, I kept saying, "Just help me. Lead me. Guide me. I can't do this any more." And then I felt better. I went back to the 7 a.m. mass the next day—and again the day after that. After a while, I began to say to myself, *I think that I love Jesus, but I don't know Him.*

Soon afterward, in September of 1999, I was in the church one Sunday morning and saw a notice about something called the Alpha course. It said, "An opportunity to learn: Who is Jesus? Why did He die? How do I pray? How do I read the Bible?" I got so excited. I thought, "I'm singing love songs to Him, and I don't even know who He is. Now I have a chance to find out."

It turned out to be the first time the church had run the

course. I managed to get a babysitter for the Thursday night and went. I didn't know what to expect, but I feared it would be a collection of rather eccentric people talking about things I couldn't understand. I walked in not knowing anyone, and within a few minutes I saw two women I knew, Sue and Betty, both of whom used to come to my exercise class. It was held in someone's home, and there were about 40 people there. The home was so beautiful, and we had this wonderful dinner, and the people were very nice and friendly. I said, "This is living—and this is free!" I mean, I would have paid hundreds of dollars for a self-help program, and this was free. We watched the first video, and I loved the way it was so normal and easy to understand.

After that first night, I looked forward to each Thursday night. I bought a Bible and had to force myself not to talk all the time in the group, because there was so much I wanted to know. I loved the videos. I could relate to everything the speaker said, and I loved his sense of humor. Our priest was the leader and he didn't talk. He just let us talk, which was great.

I was very excited about the weekend about the Holy Spirit, and the second I got there, I started crying. I thought, *Wait a minute, something must be wrong here. I can't stop crying.* I didn't know anything about the Holy Spirit, and I was a bit confused. When they prayed the prayer inviting the Holy Spirit to come, I immediately started having memories of childhood abuse. It was something which always haunted me, in the back of my mind, but I never let it out. I also felt again all the pain I had gone through at the end of my marriage. Some people started to pray for me and, as they did so, I had a vision of Jesus taking a sword out of my heart. Then I just started to cry again. It was wonderful and, as we prayed, Jesus kept leading me through the different areas of healing that needed to take place.

Throughout the course, I felt myself giving my life to God. After it was finished, I went to a "Life in the Spirit" program and a conference on the Spirit where I received the gift of tongues. I felt myself running after God. At that time, I had about 30 women coming to my exercise classes every day at 9:30 in the morning—and again two evenings a week and sometimes on weekends. I rented a studio in town and it was quite a business, but as time went on I felt I didn't really want to do it anymore. I decided to start playing Christian music during the sessions instead of the other kinds of music I used to play.

The first time I started playing the Christian music, one of the women, Lee, came up to me afterward and said, "You look happier. You look like you have peace." I told her about Alpha and about Jesus and about church. As we talked, I told her about my decision to live the single life without constantly looking for a relationship. And she said, "You can't be the same person. You're always partying till five in the morning."

I said, "I know. But I've found something new. I'm alone, and I'm happy."

And so she went to Alpha, where she was powerfully

touched by the Holy Spirit during the weekend and became a Christian. My mother has also started going to church again. I have now turned my dining room and living room into a studio and am continuing to run my aerobics class from home. I put all my trust in the Lord, and I've given my life one hundred percent to Him. My children are now in a Catholic school, and Jesus has brought so much hope and peace and love in our lives.

Until recently, deep down I really thought Jesus was just a story—a fairy tale to tell people about God. Now Jesus is my best friend, and I wake up in the morning and say, "Good morning, Jesus. How are you?" I read the Bible every day and pray non-stop, as if Jesus were sitting here with me. And He is. I know He is. All day long I say, "I give you my day. Where do You want me to go today?" I'm still friends with Jim and see him often. We're still close and get together with the children as a family. I've changed so much that I think I would be such a better wife today than I was before.

There have always been people who loved me as I have gone through these painful years of my life, but they were broken and hurt too. Now my life is so different because I have Jesus to help me.

Marie Joseph remains an active member of her local Catholic church which she describes as "my home." She recently started a new job as the computer teacher at a Catholic school where she teaches 300 children.

"My mother's marriage fell apart and she gave me away to a friend of hers... I was not allowed to sit on any of the furniture—just on the floor."

10

THE STORY OF VANESSA WENTZEL

For the first 16 years of her life, Vanessa Wentzel of Ohio, only spent two years with her mother. The other years were spent with foster parents and in a large orphanage in Pennsylvania. Here she describes how, when her life seemed at its lowest ebb, she discovered that she was loved after all.

I was born in Harrisburg, Pennsylvania, and I was placed in and out of foster care for the first five years of my life. Then my real mother decided to have me back to live with her when she got married (not to my father). A couple of years later, my mother's marriage fell apart, and she gave me away to a friend of hers—an older married woman with three grown children.

This woman didn't really want me and thought she was doing my mom a favor by taking me. She was very rich and thought she could "provide for me." She had this big beautiful home, with three or four bedrooms, but I had to sleep on the floor in the office in a sleeping bag. I had clothing and good food and things like that, but I had to follow lots of rules. I was not allowed to sit on any of the furniture—just on the floor. There was no love involved.

When I was ten, the woman said she had decided to put me into an orphanage in Hershey, Pennsylvania. She said I would see my mother for a few minutes when I was taken to the orphanage, because she was the only one who could sign the papers of authorization. I was told that I was absolutely, one hundred percent, not allowed to cry when I saw my mother because it would hurt my mother's feelings. In the end, I saw my mom for five or ten minutes, and I didn't cry. Of course, I would have if I hadn't been made to promise I wouldn't, but I was afraid to cry after what I had been told. When my mom left, I didn't see her for what seemed like years.

The orphanage was very, very big, with thousands of children covering the whole city. It was founded by Milton Hershey, the person who started the Hershey organization—Hershey Bars and things—who had realized that there was a need for people who don't want their kids. We worked on farms, we milked cows—and that milk went toward the chocolate made by Hershey.

The orphanage was broken up into many "homes," each of which had 14 children. Then there were five homes in each cluster and five clusters in each division. Each home had "house parents" who were in charge, but as you got older, you changed homes so I had many different "parents." I really enjoyed it at first, but then I noticed that other kids were getting to go home on the weekends and for Christmas—and even for two weeks in the summer. Their parents were still involved with them but just couldn't take care of them financially. I never got that. In the summer, I would go to summer camp for two weeks, and every once in a while I was invited somewhere for Christmas. Otherwise I stayed at the orphanage.

I was there for about six years, and then I started to act up in an effort to get out. I didn't do anything particularly bad, just getting home late and not doing my homework. That sort of thing. In the end I got kicked out, and my mom had no real option but to bring me home. So I went to live with her at her home in Ohio. When I got there, she just didn't know what to do with me. She didn't understand that I had grown up and just said, "I'm your mother, you're my daughter and you're going to do what I say." There was no relationship. She had been an orphan herself and didn't know how to break the cycle.

Soon afterward, I found myself as a pregnant teen. I was at a party with my boyfriend and became intoxicated. I hadn't heard of "date rape" at that time, so I just figured I deserved it because I had gotten drunk. I decided to keep the child and on February 15, 1985, I had a beautiful baby girl named Candice Marie. After she was born, my mother told me again and again that I was not going to be a good mother, and the best thing for me to do would be to give the baby away. That is what she had done, and it would be best for me. She convinced me it was the right thing to do and then suggested a plan. She said I should go with some of her friends out to dinner, and when I came back Candice would be gone. And that's what we did. Candice was six months old and was given away to an acquaintance of my mother's. I never saw her again.

I was terribly upset at what had happened. I left my mother and started traveling. I went to Indiana, New York, Myrtle Beach, Florida, California, and Las Vegas. I lived in all these places. I lived in each one for maybe six months and was constantly looking for a man to come into my life and give me a "real" family. In 1989 I met a man in South Carolina, but our relationship didn't last long.

On September 22 of that year, Hurricane Hugo came. The National Guard knocked on everybody's doors and put us all on buses and took us inland, away from the ocean. When we got back to our homes, it was just a scene of disaster. Everything was gone, gone. Even the place where I worked as a waitress was gone.

Throughout my life, I have always tried to reach out to mom, to try to have that bond, so I called her to see if I could go back to her for a while. By now she had remarried. They thought about it for a couple of weeks and then said yes. Shortly after arriving in Ohio, I discovered I was pregnant. Several conversations with the father left me to bear yet another child alone. My mother's response, of course, was, "How could you do this to me?"

I had my baby—a boy named Lynndon Chad—and moved out soon afterward. I was determined to keep Lynndon, and he was my joy! As the years passed, I cared for him while doing lots of different jobs. I married and divorced twice, still looking for love, not yet realizing it was right before me. My son taught me unconditional love, and I learned so much.

In May of 2000, my then boyfriend and I decided to marry. I moved in with him and gave up everything: my home, my job, everything we knew as solid. We had lived in North Canton, Ohio, since Lynndon was in first grade. Lynndon was very excited too, because he was going to have a dad. We moved to Stone Creek, Ohio, which is about 45 minutes away from where we were, and a couple of months after we moved in I became pregnant. We were delighted! I had always wanted another child, and Lynndon wanted siblings. It just made our plans for a September wedding all the more exciting.

Then, three weeks before our wedding day, my husband-to-be walked out. I came home from work one day to find he had disconnected all the utilities and taken everything, including food, and left. Lynndon found a message on the answering machine from my fiancé saying that he wasn't coming home. He was five or six years younger than me, and with me pregnant, I am sure it was a lot of pressure for him. But it came as a terrible blow to me. I called a friend and I cried, and then the next day it was like, "OK, what do I do now?"

So in August 2000, we moved back in with my mom, which was not an easy thing to do. I was in a terrible situation. My life had just fallen apart; I had another child on the way; I was living with my mother; I was only working part time and couldn't find a substantial job because I was pregnant. So my last resort was to go to church. I had tried different churches occasionally in my life, but I had never found one which seemed to be interested in teaching me about Christianity. But I had a friend named Lara who went to church at Mount Tabor United Methodist in East Canton, and I had gone a couple of times before.

This time I took Lynndon, and he sat in the pew and cried because he was so confused. He didn't understand anything about what was happening. He would ask, "How do I know when to sit? How do I know when to stand? How do I know what we're singing?" He had no idea. But the church was very welcoming and gave me a "Welcome Cup" as we went in—something they were giving to new people containing brochures about the church and what they had to offer. Inside the cup was a brochure about something called the Alpha course, which it said was an introduction to Christianity. I took a look and thought, *That might be for me.*

We went back to the church the following Sunday, and I started going to the Sunday School in the mornings. And there, my teacher told me about Alpha and suggested I go. So I went to the first session of the course on a Monday night and sat down to dinner in the fellowship hall with quite a lot of people. We watched the video and I liked it. I am the kind of person who loves to take notes, and I took a lot of notes. I took Lynndon with me, and he went to the childcare and loved it. Suddenly it wasn't like walking into a church; it was like walking into somebody's home.

In the small group, I had lots of questions. Things like, "If this God is going to provide for me then why do I have to pray? Why do I have to talk to Him if He knows what I want?" Sometime in the past I had seen some evangelist on TV, and I had said some kind of prayer asking Jesus into my life, but nothing ever happened. I had expected to feel something, but I didn't—so I had questions about that. I kept going back week after week—and one thing that kept me going back was that nobody called me on the odd weeks when I didn't come. If they had phoned me and pressured me, pushing God down my throat, there is no way I would have gone back. I felt it was a safe place for me to go. I was bored, I was fat, I was pregnant, I couldn't work, and it was a way for me to get out of the house, get a free meal, get free childcare, and get interaction with other people. It was a night out for me.

As time went on, I read the book *Searching Issues*, which for me was the most wonderful tool in helping me to faith. It covered all the questions I had one after the other, and I became more and more convinced. I couldn't make the retreat because my mom got ill, and I had to take care of her, so they organized a special night just for me, and we watched the video *How Can I Be Filled with the Holy*

Spirit? Afterward, they prayed for me, and I thought I felt the Holy Spirit as they did so. Then I went home and began thinking about things a bit more. I kept going on Monday nights and on Sundays, and I started to really study and learn. I started to get my questions answered.

Then something terrible happened. The day after Christmas I went in for a routine doctor's visit for my baby. I was seven months pregnant and it was just a routine visit. The doctor tried to hear the heart beat and couldn't hear anything. Then they did an ultrasound, by which time I was getting worried. I didn't look at the screen because I was afraid. I just lay there and prayed, saying, "God, please don't let this happen to me. Please don't take my baby from me. Please have mercy on me. I can't handle this right now."

But it wasn't to be. They took me back into the doctor's office, and she came in and told me that my son had died. She then said she would leave me to have some time to myself, and I said to God at that moment, "I can't handle this." Then I basically called God's bluff. And I said "OK, they say just turn my life over to You and You can take care of everything . . . then fine, here, take it 'cause I can't do this anymore." I had just had it. "I can't do this anymore, and if You're going to prove it to me, now is the time to do it."

I went into the hospital the next day, and all I had to do was hurt. All I had to do was feel the pain. My labor was induced, and I was in labor for four days, which was awful, awful, awful. Several of the nurses were Christians, however, and they would come in and pray with me and have lunch with me. They were unbelievable, but they kept telling me that I was the one who inspired them because by now my faith had become so strong. It was at that time that I realized that when I had given my life over to Christ, He had taken it.

It doesn't make the pain go away. It doesn't make the pain go away at all. But it does make it so much easier to bear. I think I have now learned the difference between suffering with God and self-destruction. There is such a big difference there. In the end it was still not going well, and they decided to give me a C-Section. Before they took me into surgery, the nurses and my church friends all put their hands on me and prayed for me. Even Lynndon, who is ten, prayed for me, out loud with everyone else there. He just opened his mouth and out came the most beautiful, beautiful words, adult words—comforting words. At that moment I knew that I would be OK.

I had the C-section on December 30 and my son, Lane Christian, was born. He was stillborn, but he was beautiful and he was mine. I had him baptized in a bedside service in my hospital room surrounded by church friends and family. A week later we had a funeral for him, and we buried him. Throughout this time, people just surrounded me with love. I didn't have to worry about the funeral or expenses. Everything was taken care of for me. My Sunday School teacher even wrote Lane's obituary which, I imagine, was quite hard for him considering he and his wife had experienced a loss as well.

I know I have changed. I think I would be in a loony bin

right now after losing my son. But I now know it is OK to feel the pain. It's OK to get on my knees and cry out to God and say, "It hurts. Help me."

I've gone through a lot of stages, but I've had the support of my congregation and the support of God through the Holy Spirit. Where my mom is concerned, I have finally realized after 33 years that I love my mother, but I can no longer help her myself. And I'm sure she has seen the change in me. I have so much more patience now, and I don't get upset with her in the way that I used to.

For 33 years all I have wanted has been my mother's love and approval. Now I don't need her approval in the same way. I've got all the love and approval I need from God.

I didn't understand the difference between God and Jesus before. I thought Jesus was a person like you and me who was a preacher who lived long ago. But now Jesus is my lifeline. It's like before I might have been shaking hands with Jesus, but now I'm holding on for dear life, and I'm not going to let Him go.

Vanessa now lives in Smyrna, Tennessee, where she is a member of her local United Methodist church. She has become involved in work with teenage parents at their schools. Her mother is now attending weekly Bible studies. Vanessa says: "She has accepted my faith and I have accepted her love!"

"Throughout my army career, I don't recall ever having cried. Not even in Vietnam, seeing so many with arms and legs blown off— bodies mangled and dead. No, not a tear…"

THE STORY OF BOB CAMPBELL

Vietnam veteran Bob Campbell saw his family disintegrate as a result of his hard drinking and abusive lifestyle as a First Sergeant in the U.S. Army. Despite finding some success in business, he remained an alcoholic, drinking scotch from 6:30 in the morning until 8 at night. Then one day in January 1998, everything changed.

I was in the army for 22 years and for many years was a senior non-commissioned officer, a rank which is often associated with very hard people—and, for the most part, justifiably so. I was very abusive to folks, which was part of the job, and it would filter down to my family as well. The abuse, along with the drinking and carousing, was part of normal life. It may be a stereotype, but that was the lifestyle. I was an alcoholic for probably 12 or 14 years, and as a result of my lifestyle (a lifestyle that didn't include God) our family went into shambles.

On the day that I retired from the army, my wife and kids were supposed to be at the parade, with all the pomp and circumstance, but they didn't show. When I came home from the retirement ceremonies, there was nothing left. The family had gone. I put the police on alert, because I didn't know what might have happened. But after a day or two, it became clear that my wife had taken my two children and walked out. She had never said anything either to me or to the children about what she was going to do. Part of the reason was "Dad's the abusive type and we're tired of that." That was 1979, my son's last year of high school, so he would have been 18 and my daughter 17.

With that divorce came the separation of my son, Keith, and myself. He sided more with his mother. She moved to Florida, and Keith went out on his own and became the drinking and carousing type, just like his father. He fell back on the old lifestyle. In the end, my wife remarried, and the children kind of lost touch with her as well. For me, it was a crisis situation when they left. I'd lost the family, newly retired, and I started going through A.A. (Alcoholics Anonymous) with my drinking problem, which was good for me.

In 1989, I started my own desk-top video conferencing company. We were the first desk-top video conferencing business that provided good TV quality instead of the herky, jerky 30 frames-per-second kind of a product. It was quite exciting, and we built the company so fast that in 1995 a publicly-traded company took a look at us and bought us. They purchased the company, and I made a tremendous amount of money. The stock went from 60 cents a share to being worth more than four dollars a share in a few short weeks. With ownership of three million shares, I made a lot of money.

At this time I didn't see my children very often—my daughter more so, but Keith was still very distant, and their mother was still in Florida. Then, seven months later, came another crisis situation when the Security Exchange Commission shut the company down. I was no longer in the company, but I was still a major shareholder.

It turned out that the men who had bought the company were fraudulent. It was the first case of internet fraud—of hyping stock and then selling it. I had sold some stock, but the rest went way down in value. To make matters worse, for the next two years I was under investigation by the FBI because I had sold the company to these fraudulent people. So that sent me into another drinking frenzy all over again. You can imagine. Though the Justice Department eventually determined that I was not at fault, I was very bitter against the people I had sold to. It took me back into the old Bob lifestyle of drinking and cheating and hating—all those things.

I was going through all this when I saw my son on Thanksgiving Day 1997 and he said, "Dad, can you get away for a couple of days? I need to talk with you." He suggested going off to play golf together. I knew my son was very bitter towards me, and I was very, very surprised that he would suggest this. He'd never called me up before to say he wanted to spend time with me. He was only recently married, and I thought there must be something terribly wrong with the marriage. I had visited them once and had seen that he was drinking and living the old lifestyle I had lived. When the time came, we left in the car for Ocean City on the Maryland coast. Keith was driving my car, and he turned and said to me, "Dad, do you know how to pray?" I was scared to death. I was sure there was a problem in their marriage. But before I could answer, he said, "Dad, well, I have found Jesus Christ."

I said, "What?"

He said, "Yeah, that's why I wanted to take a couple of days to tell you about it."

He told me he had been to something called an Alpha course at his local church. And for the three days all we talked about was Alpha and what a difference it had made. You could see the big change in Keith. If it had been the old Keith it would have been a drinking holiday, but it wasn't. And his language had changed. His whole outlook on life, on other people . . . the forgiveness in his heart. I thought, *Gosh, he must have found something.*

He invited me to the next session of Alpha which was four months out. All this time I was at the Justice Department acting as a witness on behalf of the government and just drinking myself into oblivion. But I finally straightened myself up enough to go to the course in January of 1998, at St. Louis Catholic Church in Clarksville, Maryland.

On the first night we watched the video, and at the end the speaker gave us the chance to thank God, ask Him for forgiveness, and to turn our hearts to Him. I wanted to do it that night, but I didn't. I thought about it all the next week. But I didn't do it on the second week either. Then, on the third session, I gave my heart to God.

From that point my life changed. I asked God's forgiveness of all my sins and invited Him to come into my heart, to take away all my old desires, and make me new. That night the old Bob went away. Up to that moment, I was drinking scotch from 6:30 in the morning until 8 at night. But after that third session, I didn't drink again—and I haven't to this day.

I know that much of the old Bob has changed. The Spirit of our Lord has mellowed me and given me a new, more loving, forgiving, and caring spirit. Also gone is any desire to participate in any of the old ways of life. In fact, I don't even like to talk about it. I've lost nothing of true value, and I'm no longer looking for something. I've already found it in a personal relationship with Jesus Christ. Because of this new-found relationship and daily reading of the Bible, I see the goodness, faithfulness, and protection of God in so many ways. It's like standing on the shoulders of a giant.

Throughout my army career, I don't recall ever having

cried. Not even in Vietnam, seeing so many with arms and legs blown off—bodies mangled and dead. No, not a tear then. But now there are tears often. They come when I pray for others or talk to other Christians about the goodness of the Lord.

Bob Campbell has since helped on several Alpha courses at St. Louis' Catholic Church, Clarksville.

11

THE STORY OF RAY LEWANDOWSKI

Ray Lewandowski of Bellevue, Washington, thought he had fulfilled the American dream. He had a beautiful wife, two children, a successful job, a high income, a large house, and "all the toys." Then it all began to fall apart. Here he tells how his attitudes changed on a local Alpha course.

I was raised in a devout Polish Catholic neighborhood near Chicago. As a child, church for me meant wearing uncomfortable clothes, sitting up straight, and listening to services that didn't mean a lot. Even worse, I believed that

173

if I did not live my life exactly how the priest told me to, I would go to hell. When I was 13, I stopped going.

I studied Marketing and Business Administration at Illinois State University in Bloomington, Illinois, funding my education by throwing parties. There would be anywhere from 200 to 1,500 people attending each weekend, and we would charge $3 for guys and $2 for girls for beer. The beer distributor delivered directly to my apartment, and we would put a fence around the parking lot of the apartment building—and we would hold the parties there. I've always been a very driven person, always striving to be number one, living life to the fullest. I threw the best parties in town: plenty of beer and people of the opposite sex. I don't know what made them the best, but they seemed to be the biggest and the best on campus because they had to be; that was the goal. I made anything from $500 to $1,500 a week doing that, which for a student was great.

At the end of college, I went traveling to Europe and met a girl named Jennifer on a train in Germany. She was from Seattle and after two years living together and some ups and downs, we were married in St. James' Catholic Cathedral in Seattle. Neither of us was a practicing Catholic. For me, I just wanted to be married in the biggest, grandest place possible. It was all about image. We appeared to be the perfect couple. In 1992 we had a child, R.J. (Ray Junior), and then in 1994 we had another son, Alex.

By then I had been a successful stockbroker and moved on to managing a mortgage company branch. The goal was to be living the American dream and to have it all. I was quickly attaining that dream. I made a list of everything I wanted and by 1997 I had achieved everything on that list. I had a successful job, a fantastic income, a beautiful wife, children, a big house—all the toys, all the jewels, all the clothes, all the material things you could ask for. Then within a week of realizing that goal, my whole life came crashing down.

I came home from the office one night and my wife said we needed to talk. She was very unhappy, and as it turned out she was having an extra-marital affair with another woman. Within six months we were divorced. All of our family and friends were shocked. We had appeared to be the perfect family; we had it all. It was all a terrible shock to me. I thought being a husband and father meant keeping my family in all the material needs they wanted. That was my primary goal, and I had achieved it. I couldn't understand what had gone wrong. I had done everything according to plan.

The divorce cost me a lot of money, and after that I focused very intently on rebuilding my fortune. I wanted to rebuild that empire—including the perfect family. I took no responsibility for what happened. I just wanted to win at all costs and build my material empire. I could beat the odds and do it on my own. I still had 50-percent custody of my children, but I thought my primary responsibility to them was to provide above and beyond what anybody else could provide financially. I spent a fair amount of time with them, but I didn't consider that important. It was all the gifts and toys and trips—not time.

In October 1998, I met a wonderful girl named Emily, who worked for the same company but lived in Atlanta. She was beautiful and way out of my league—a perfect goal and she would fit in perfectly with the new family I wanted to create. It would be better than ever. By then I was a regional vice president for the company and I swept her off her feet; we had a wonderful life. We did a lot of partying and flew all over the country. Then in February 1999 we were engaged, she moved to Seattle, and we lived together. I was back on the upswing building a better empire than ever.

We married in February 2000 in a very small ceremony. My boys loved Emily, and we lived what appeared to be a happy life until October 2001. Once again, I poured on all the jewels and BMWs and a beautiful house, providing her with more material wealth than anybody could want. In May 2000 we had started our own mortgage company. I was the president of the company, and Emily was the underwriter for the company, and it was an extreme success. We had about 25 employees. Yet again, I felt like I had achieved the American dream. I had it all, only bigger and better than the first time.

Then one day in September 2001 I came home and she said, "We need to talk." Immediately, I knew what was coming; I could feel that it was going to be the same conversation all over again. I knew Emily was struggling with being away from home. Having grown up in the south, she was away from her family and was struggling with becoming part of an instant family and having two step-children. But I wasn't ready for what came next. She said she wanted to move back to Atlanta—without me. She wanted a divorce. Financially, I was enjoying my biggest windfall, my biggest success. After going through my first divorce, I had built my life up again on exactly the same foundation. Now it looked like it was blowing up a second time. Although Emily wasn't happy, she was willing to talk. She felt terrible about what was about to happen but didn't see another solution.

So we both took about ten days off work, and we talked and talked and talked.

I said, "I'll do anything: I'll move back to Atlanta with you, I'll close the company, I'll do whatever it takes." I did not want to lose again. But that wasn't enough. She said she didn't love me, she didn't trust me, and she wasn't happy. How could anyone be unhappy? We had it all. After those ten days all our friends who knew about the situation told me, "You know you've got to give up. You've got to let her go. You've got to move on."

At that point I looked deeper inside myself and thought, *This plan I have in place, this foundation I've built my life on—there's something missing. There's something not there. It's not working. My world is imploding again.* I'd gotten to where I thought I had the whole world in the palm of my hand, and it had turned into a failure.

At the end of those ten days, I was driving by a church close to our home called Westminster Chapel, when I thought, *I've tried everything else and nothing worked, so*

I'd look for help there. I called Emily on my cellphone and said, "I know it appears that our relationship's over, but would you be willing to meet with the senior pastor of this church with me? I've decided I want to explore faith, and I'd like the pastor to have an idea of my background, even if you leave." And she agreed to that. So in September 2001, we met with Pastor Gary Gulbranson, and within an hour and a half he had encouraged Emily to wait a little longer. Gary helped her understand she was not a bad person, and it was normal to feel empty and alone, given the life we were leading. Instead of moving back to Atlanta, she agreed to move into a separate apartment locally, in the Bellevue, Washington area. The pastor agreed to counsel us every couple of weeks, but only if we agreed that our ultimate goal was to save our marriage. He also highly recommended that we do an Alpha course, which was starting ten days later.

I'd never heard of Alpha at all. He said it was kind of a Christianity 101 course. It would help explain what faith was and answer any questions. I didn't understand what that had to do with saving my marriage, but I was willing to try anything. So Emily moved out into the apartment at the beginning of October, and we started the Alpha classes, which were on Sunday mornings, almost at once.

On the first day of Alpha we arranged to meet up beforehand and walk in together as a married couple. We didn't want anyone to know we were living separately. Image was still important. There were about 30 people attending the course, and the first thing that I noticed was how incredibly nice everybody was. They provided break-fast, then we had the video, then a small group discussion. At that first session I had a lot of hurt, but the course at once gave me hope. Emily and I were in the same group, which was a very inviting, warm, and open environment. Emily definitely liked the first week, so we went back the following week. I very much enjoyed the videos. Nicky Gumbel [the Alpha course speaker] has an amazingly down-to-earth, friendly way of explaining Christianity.

As the weeks went on, Emily and I began talking together on a different level, and we found ourselves spending more time together. It seemed like week by week the tapes spoke exactly about the issues or the conflicts that we were having, either in our own lives or as a couple. In a matter of six weeks—from the beginning of October to some time in November—our lives had changed so much, moving increasingly from the physical, materialistic world to a world of faith. By November, we were sharing things about ourselves—our pasts, our upbringing, and our beliefs—that we had never shared or trusted with another human in our lives. Our relationship was blossoming and within two weeks of her moving out, she was occasionally staying back at our house, and I stayed a couple of times at the apartment. Within a month we had discovered not only a love for God but a love for each other.

In fact, I discovered what love was. I didn't know what love was previous to that. An entirely new world was open-ing up to me that I never knew existed, and it was warm and filled with love. Sometime during the first few weeks of

Alpha, I said a prayer inviting God into my life. As soon as that happened, I started praying for Emily to do the same. Soon after that, Emily went on a woman's retreat and called me from there. She was with another member of our Alpha small group and said, "I've given my life to Christ." And we cried. One day in mid-November, I noticed that Emily had come in to work wearing her engagement ring, which she had stopped wearing when we split up. I noticed it immediately and told her so. Once again, I cried. We now seemed to have a love for each other which was deeper than either one of us had ever experienced.

At that time, Emily moved back home. We had been apart for six weeks. After that Pastor Ralph, who was in charge of our Alpha course, started meeting with me weekly, having breakfast, mentoring me, helping me build my faith, helping me pray, helping me study the Bible. I felt my goals, aspirations, and focus start to change. Things that were everything to me before—like what kind of car I drove, how much money I had or my status in life—didn't seem to matter. On July 9, 2002, Emily gave birth to a daughter, who was conceived on the Alpha retreat weekend. Lucy, our daughter, is an amazing blessing.

Now I read the Bible daily, I pray, and my relationship with my two sons has blossomed. I am currently attending my fourth Alpha series as a table leader. I now understand that it isn't riches people desire; it's my time and my heart they want. Honest love and compassion is always better than a "win at all costs" attitude. And Emily has also changed dramatically. She loves God with all her heart and, through God, we have learned how to love each other. Now we pray together, which we would never have done before. My attitude toward my first wife Jennifer has changed too. Some months ago, I called her and apologized for my part in the break-up of our marriage and told her that through God I have found out what love is.

Before Alpha I probably thought Jesus was a historical figure. I believed in Jesus, but I really didn't know who He was. Now Jesus is my world. One of the biggest lessons that Alpha taught me is that religion is not a place or a church, but a personal relationship with Jesus Christ. He is the foundation of my life.

In August 2002 Ray and Emily Lewandowski were baptized in a local river by their pastor. They have helped on several Alpha courses. Ray says, "We want to share God's Word to the ends of the earth. We owe Him everything."

THE ALPHA COURSE

The Alpha course provides an opportunity to explore the meaning of life. For more information on Alpha, or to purchase resources, contact the following:

Alpha U.S.A.
74 Trinity Place
New York, NY 10006
Tel: 800 DO ALPHA
Tel: 800.362.5742
Fax: 212.406.7521
e-mail: info@alphausa.org
www.alphausa.org

Alpha Canada
1620 W. 8th Ave., Suite 300
Vancouver, BC V6J 1V4
Tel: 800.743.0899
Fax: 604.224.6124
e-mail: office@alphacanada.org
www.alphacanada.org

To purchase resources in Canada:

Cook Communications Ministries
P.O. Box 98, 55 Woodslee Avenue
Paris, ONT N3L 3E5
Tel: 800.263.2664
Fax: 800.461.8575
e-mail: custserv@cook.ca
www.cook.ca